Maryann Karinch

PHOTOGRAPHS BY DAVID BROOKS

the

Lessons

EXTREME ATHLETES SHOW YOU HOW

from the Edge

TO TAKE ON HIGH RISK AND SUCCEED

A FIRESIDE BOOK
Published By Simon & Schuster
New York London Toronto Sydney Singapore

FIRESIDE
Rockefeller Center
1230 Avenue of the Americas
New York, NY 10020

FIRESIDE and colophon are registered trademarks
of Simon & Schuster, Inc.

Designed by Ruth Lee

Manufactured in the United States of America

10   9   8   7   6   5   4   3   2   1

Library of Congress Cataloging-in-Publication Data

Karinch, Maryann.
Lessons from the edge : extreme athletes show you how to take on high risk and succeed /
Maryann Karinch ; photographs by David Brooks.
p.   cm.
"A Fireside Book."
1. Athletes—Training of. 2. Extreme sports. I. Title.

GV711.5 .K37 2000
613.7'1—dc21
99-057396
ISBN 0-684-86215-8

Acknowledgments

Thank you to my loving partner, Jim McCormick, a man who lives his philosophy of risk taking and generously shares his talents with people around him. He contributed to this project in many practical ways, from ideas through emotional support. And, as usual, my mother and brother provided great thoughts as well as love and prayers from the moment I began this effort. Thank you to action photographer David Brooks, his supportive wife, Cindy, and lovely daughters, Brittany and Kaitlin. Having David as an artistic partner on this book involved the unflagging support of his entire family, who missed him so much as he lugged his camera gear from airport to airport, slope to slope, and river to river. He is a truly gifted and dedicated professional and, now, a great friend. I thank him for his talent and for his patience. Thanks also to Patrick Avon for bringing us together. I am also indebted to my caring and capable agent, Laura Belt of Adler and Robin Books, and my editors at Simon and Schuster: Sarah Baker, who paved the way for this effort, and Tricia Medved, whose commitment of her talent to this book helped take it to greater heights. Tricia really made a difference. Thanks also to Anne Bartholomew at S&S, who helped me in many ways.

And what would this book be without the amazing athletes who talked to me at length and in depth about their passion, successes, disappointments, and the lessons they learned in life! They have big hearts, sharp minds, and inspiring dreams. I am also grateful to the people who helped me contact the athletes: Franz Weber Sports Management and Consulting, Gary Speer of the Flyaway Wind Tunnels, Bob McClellan of McClellan Sports Management Group, Ann Krcik of Extreme Connection, Nadia Guerriero of Gold Medal Management, Jeff Beckham and his Web site, www.greatoutdoors.com, Ann Meizel, Lori Hall at CSM, Cheryl Lynch of Lynch Archer, Sarah Hall of Sarah Hall Productions, the One Step Beyond agency, Travis Chipras at Specialized, Steve Blick and Gabey Browning at GT, Greg Stokes at Oakley, David Hoffman, and Jeanne Hoffman.

Thank you to the experts who contributed processes, exercises, interpretations, and recommendations that have helped the athletes in this book and are sure to help readers; these people are my virtual board of advisors: Joyah French, Anna Wise, Jack Phillips, Dr. Bob Moore, Dr. Scott Connelly, Christine Ely, Dr. Leslie Anderson, Kevin Maselka, John Lull, Chris Robinson, Todd Offenbacher, Dr. James Canton, Aaron Bethlenfalvy, and the folks at California Canoe and Kayak and United States Parachute Association. I also appreciate the special assistance that Bob Garrow, Karen Deichman, Mark Hayden, and Rob Drynan of Cougar Mountain Adventures in Whistler gave both David Brooks and me. Thanks also to skiers Eric Pehota, Dan Treadway, and Wendy Brookbank for their willingness to participate in our photo shoots despite bad weather.

The photographers who shared their photos of unusual moments also contributed so much: Kurt Issel, freeflying; Tracy St. John, adventure racing; Michael Powers, extreme sea kayaking; Shelley Eades, Jim McCormick's skydive into Candlestick (3com) Park; Tyler Young, Paragliding; and Kennan Harvey, Steph Davis's ascent of Shipton Spire in Pakistan. Thanks also to Capital Color's Mike Langford and David Rockwell for excellent processing services. Thank you also to the people whose hospitality made some key photographs possible and information available: the folks at Woodward Camp in Pennsylvania; Sally Carmichael, Susan Darch, and Laura Street of the Whistler Resort Association, Whistler/Blackcomb; Keith Green, Nazareth Speedway; Adam Sahl, Indy Light PR; Josh Krulewitz at ESPN; and Kevin Monaghan at NBC.

I want to also acknowledge the contribution of my old adventure racing buddies on Team MET-Rx, Jim Newman, Knute Neihoff, Jimmy McElroy, and Jim Coddington, whose skill and spirit made for extreme fun no matter how awful we felt on the trail. And thanks to my new extreme pals, the members of the Miramar Beach Kayak Club.

For Jim, Mom, Karl

and all the other adventurers and champions in my life

And in memory of Alex Lowe

Adventurers of all kinds will always hear the music of your spirit

Contents

Lessons from the Edge

Introduction

Fans of extreme sports who discovered I was writing this book offered descriptions of "sick tricks" and "rad contests." I said, "Thanks, but this book is about what amazing athletes have to say." I asked these winners, adventurers, and world record holders to tell me what they do, how they do it, and how their ideas can benefit all of us. They did so in great detail and with a generous spirit.

The interviews for this book were the culmination of four years of learning about extreme beings. Before I did my first adventure race in 1995, the inaugural Eco-Challenge in Utah, I sent questionnaires to every registered competitor. I planned to do articles about the race and wanted insights about why people wanted to do something so full of deprivation and pain and how they were preparing for it. After completing the race—our Team MET-Rx was one of only twenty-one that finished—and doing follow-up with some of the other competitors, I became intrigued with the other athletes' success secrets. In fact, I realized our team had a few good ones, too. Thanks to the openness of some tremendous athletes and a few more competitive challenges of my own, my knowledge of extreme sports deepened over the next few years and here we are.

Great athletes have told me so many gripping, thrilling, and beautiful stories that I am now a more interesting dinner guest. I have woven pieces of some stories throughout the book, and used others between chapters to highlight the "lessons from the edge" in action.

Sometimes the athletes also pointed me toward experts and books that profoundly impacted their performance and thinking—and thinking is a big part of extreme sports. Don't leave your brain behind if you love taking physical risks. I've found that many people assume it takes a certain level of intelligence and problem-solving ability to summit Everest and return, but they don't assign the same need to doing skateboarding tricks in the halfpipe. If you're one of those people, this book will surprise you.

Here's one more thing that may surprise you: nearly everyone talked about trusting a "gut feeling"—intuition. This brings up an interesting question. What came first, the intuition or the risk taking? Were they born with a keen ability to sense when to try something dangerous and how to do it successfully? Read the book and let me know what you think. What I know for sure is that they told me the "sixth sense" is like a muscle. It gets stronger with use.

So if I had to make a couple of basic recommendations to someone who wants to model the great athletes who contributed to this book, I'd say, practice thinking through contingencies and get used to listening to your inner voice. Do it when you're about to do something normal like drive on the freeway or interview for a new job. Then, when you pick a scary line in the backcountry, you'll be better prepared.

Finally, however you decide to apply the lessons in these pages, please heed the words of a great adventurer, sailing world record holder and wise man Gerard Fusil: "You won't do well if you're just out to impress somebody. Do what you love in the deepest part of yourself."

"Without adventure, civilization is in full decay."

—ALFRED NORTH WHITEHEAD, PHILOSOPHER

"Some people have 'hang out' genes and others have 'do stuff' genes."

—T. J. LAVIN, FREESTYLE BIKER

FAME and wealth belong to great quarterbacks, center forwards, and home run hitters. Society prizes them like the Romans cheered gladiators who crushed their opponent's skull. They're heroes because they win.

Extreme athletes are heroes because they *try*—something harder, faster, longer. Anyone can benefit from their insights and relate to them as people. Their goal is often not a score or a medal. In some sports, those widely acknowledged as the greatest never even compete. Money doesn't lure them to the edge, either; multimillion-dollar contracts do not yet beckon most extreme athletes. The prize they want is the full-bodied thrill of accomplishment and the lessons they offer you are how to achieve it.

CHAPTER 1

What Do You Have in Common with Extreme Athletes?

The hunger to be really good at something runs through all of us. It's normal to crave the satisfaction and sense of self-worth that come from success. No one would question the sanity of wanting to perform well consistently and be cool under pressure. All of these urges are key catalysts for extreme athletes as well as people who don't venture near the edge.

There is also something we'd all like to have in common with extreme athletes. The best have developed and discovered techniques that repeatedly deliver the desired results in the face of uncommon challenges. Chances are very good that their tips on mental focus and physical fitness will boost your abilities even if planting a flag on Everest's summit or rotating 900 degrees on a skateboard are not in your plans. They will help you be a little bit more amazing.

A lot of times, extreme athletes inspire us by merely surviving, and sometimes it looks like they must have magical powers to do that. They don't. They know how to run through their options consciously and consistently. That's the first lesson.

A Glimpse at Living on the Edge

Extreme athletes have to develop the skill of effectively evaluating their options because they have a different way of looking at the world. Where other people see only danger, they also see fun. They look for risk in life. People who have this point of view, but don't have contingencies in mind when the unexpected happens, don't last long. For the athletes who do, it's perfectly reasonable to defy conventional wisdom about where and how to have a good time.

The Tsunami Rangers have been doing it since 1984. They

paddle at places like Pigeon Point, which juts into the ocean fifty miles south of San Francisco. At the tip is a 115-foot-tall lighthouse built in the days of wooden ships to warn mariners of dangers like rock reefs, which are at or below water level depending on the tide. The hazards those sailors tried to avoid are a playground for the Rangers, a tribe of extreme sea kayakers with Kevlar-armored boats.

Just because they've been paddling in isolated surf zones, complex rock gardens, and dark sea caves for years, however, doesn't mean the risk is gone. Of all the environments where extreme athletes play, the sea offers the most surprises. Chaos is the norm. What the years have given the Tsunami Rangers is not less risk, but rather more practice thinking through options when the unexpected does happen— like the spring afternoon when a large, breaking wave came around the corner at Pigeon Point and confronted Ranger Eric Soares.

> I was inside the corner, unaware of the size of the wave. It was about fifteen feet high. I knew there was no way I could get away from it. Normally, if you think you're going to hit something, you bail out and swim like a seal. This time, I was trapped.

The day before the incident, Eric and Jim Kakuk, cofounders of the Tsunami Rangers, had speculated about what to do if they knew that a wave would slam them against the rocks. Jim's river kayaking background told him to lean toward the obstacle to avoid being pinned against it. He reconsidered. No, he concluded, the ocean withdraws after the wave so you won't get pinned. The greater danger is having your body smashed into the cliff. Lean into the wave; go hull-first into the rocks.

> "Hull-first, hull-first." That's all I thought. I had to use my boat as a pad. As the wave hit me, I leaned into it doing a low brace. I had on a helmet and wetsuit, but no gloves. Wish I'd had gloves. I leaned

into the wave to try and use it as a cushion. Then I hit the reef—bam, bam, bam, I started bouncing on it. It was like a road with rocks in it. As I was bouncing, I was relaxing—conserving my energy so I had everything I needed when I hit the cliff.

I looked at my paddle blade and saw it break off. I was riding on the shaft. It was scraping along and grinding on the reef and getting closer and closer to my hand. I was hoping it wouldn't wear away completely because my hand would be next. I knew I'd have to use my hand if it came to that to protect my torso. The cliff was right in front of me. I took a breath: "Hull-first." I didn't know there was a drop-off at the end.

Suddenly, I was flying in the air, headed downward, hull-first. You don't want to be in the air with a boat. You want to be in the water. My hull took the beating. It died for me. I'd named my boat *Elendil.** I thought, what a fortuitous name.

Luckily, what hit me was a rogue wave. The rest of the waves that came in after that were not nearly as big so I was able to swim the battered boat away from danger.

> **If you're prepared for your adventure, the answer you need in a crisis will come.**

Keen self-awareness and intelligence give extreme athletes a distinct advantage in averting serious injury or death. Add to that the progress made recently in equipment, conditioning programs, and our knowledge base, and most people would probably agree that extreme

---

*In J. R. R. Tolkien's *The Lord of the Rings,* the great warrior Elendil sacrificed himself to save the world from the evil Sauron.

ERIC SOARES BRACES IN SURF TO AVOID CAPSIZING.

sports—activities in which failure of mind, body, or gear can have devastating consequences—are not necessarily the domain of wild-eyed asylum escapees.

What Is the Nature of Extreme Sports?

Extreme sports are competitive as well as noncompetitive adventures, such as high-altitude mountaineering. Stunts are just part of the backdrop; some of the athletes featured in this book do scary maneuvers for movies, but these experiences are not the focus of their lives as athletes. As a corollary, doing something outrageous once and walking away does not make a person a great extreme athlete or a credible source of advice.

Some of the competitive sports like bicycle stunt riding and aggressive in-line street skating were not spectator-ready until ESPN's X Games and NBC's Gravity Games, for example, imposed a structure that worked on television and offered a running color commentary. These sports had a history of camaraderie and contests, but not high-profile competitions, when ESPN brought them to TV audiences in 1995. Prior to that, the challenge for the uninitiated public was that the athletes' objectives were not intuitively obvious. (Even those who can't explain what happens between the commercials during a football game know the ball should cross the line.)

Competitive freestyle events are not institutionalized, rule-bound sports, so it follows that their nature is to deviate from the expected. In skysurfing, competitors *try* to spin upside down. Rodeo kayakers *want* to get stuck in suckholes. Freestyle bikers *must* get off the saddle to do tricks.

Increasingly, the best introduction to extreme sports, as well as the most intense coverage for fans, is on the Internet (see Appendix A).

Web sites offer real-time details in multimedia and links to explanations so viewers can log on anytime to feel the challenge, grasp the objectives, know the players, and learn the vocabulary. For example, www.quokka.com's coverage of the grueling and successful first attempt by Mark Synnott, Jared Ogden, and Alex Lowe to free-climb the Northwest Face of Great Trango Tower in Pakistan* in July 1999 featured daily voice mails from the climbers, detailed maps, time-lapse photographs, and much more.

Extreme sports can be categorized in a number of ways, none of which perfectly introduces them. First, they could be discussed in terms of the gear they require; most depend on boards, wheels, ropes, or boats. Not all of them do, though. In some cases, like the Marathon des Sables, a 150-mile race across the Moroccan desert, the main elements are the athlete and the environment.

Classifying the sports according to where they occur—snow, ice, rock, raging water, air, skate parks—has value because it implies the strong connection that the athletes have with their chosen venue. On the other hand, it glides past the fact that many sports, by their nature, combine environments.

Finally, extreme sports can be discussed in terms of the main requirement of the activity, that is, what physical limits the athletes must stretch—speed, balance, timing, and endurance. Using this approach accents what very different extreme sports, and the athletes who do them, have in common. It also lays the foundation for discussions of cross training and reveals why some extreme athletes are superior performers in seemingly unrelated activities.

Speed In these events, the object is to be the first to finish. Style, smiles, and outfits don't matter. Picabo Street, Olympic gold medal skier:

*Todd Skinner's 1995 first ascent of Nameless Tower, aka Trango Tower, is described in later chapters.

AT SIXTY MILES AN HOUR, LUGER MICHAEL SHANNON BREAKS THE SPEED LIMIT ON A WINDING WEST VIRGINIA HILL.

It's the clock from start to finish line. No foul points. Fastest one to the bottom wins. Going eighty miles an hour, you don't have time to care about whether someone dug the way you made that turn.

Speed skiing, mountain bike racing, and many other competitive speed events are extreme because they combine the need to go fast with unforgiving terrain. In ESPN's Winter X Games, the danger of speed on whoop-dee-doos (i.e., a tight sequence of jumps) and banked turns in the skiercross, boardercross, and bikercross events is amplified by the fact that competitors are six abreast at the start. Other speed sports are extreme because the rate and levels of acceleration create a hazardous condition. Top-fuel boat and car racing, stand-up skateboarding, and street luge fall into this category.

Balance and Timing In these events, well-timed moves and exquisite body control mean the difference between a joyride and an ambulance ride. This is what skydiving while standing on a board and soaring over hills on a pint-sized BMX stunt bike have in common. In both skysurfing and freestyle biking, even the most basic tricks demand keen mental and physical abilities.

The list of extreme sports with a core requirement to push the limits of balance and timing includes big-wave surfing, extreme skiing, skateboarding, freeflying, waterfall kayaking, and many others. In fact, many extreme sports fit on that list. Speed is a key element of risk in many of them—in freeflying, the skydiver might be going 180 miles an hour, for example—but it is an integral part of the activity rather than the objective, which is extraordinary control of the body and essential gear.

Endurance Endurance events like marathons require a huge dedication to physical training and, without a doubt, the will to put one foot in front of the other repeatedly. Extreme endurance sports require more from the athlete's psyche. The intensity lasts for so long that, at some

STAR FREESTYLE BIKER T. J. LAVIN DOES A SEAT-GRAB HIGH
ABOVE THE DIRT IN LAS VEGAS.

IN A SERENE WATER SECTION OF THE GRUELING BRITISH COLUMBIA ECO-CHALLENGE, A TEAM PADDLES BESIDE SUBMERGED TREES IN THE LIL-LOOET RIVER.

point, these activities are primarily exercises in attitude, pain control, and tactical decision making. Depending on the challenge, super-fit bodies can go on and on for weeks or even months with just a little rest periodically. Succeeding in that challenge—and in some cases, that means surviving—can only happen if their minds and emotions are conditioned to support their bodies. In the words of Robert Nagle of the top adventure racing team, Eco-Internet:

> A race like ours is usually seen by people as a physical test, but in fact, it's much more an internal—that is, mental and emotional— test. The races last for so long and are replete with so many strategic and tactical decisions. How you make those decisions determines how well you do.

Why Do People Do These Things?

The answers to two main questions shed light on how extreme activities emerge and develop: Why do people do these things? and: How can they do these things and not kill themselves?

Some athletes start doing these things when they're young because they want to be different or they want an adrenaline rush. Commonly, it's a combination of both reasons; they're impulses that a lot of teenagers probably share.

Daring to Be Different Kristen Ulmer, who made the first female descent of Grant Teton, rose to fame skiing off cliffs for movies while she was still in college. In those days, she did unusual stunts so she would be noticed:

> When I first started, I just wanted to get attention by taking lots and lots of risks. Everyone was asking me if I was afraid of dying and I

just got a kick out of it. I wasn't aware that I could get hurt. . . .

The first stunt I ever did for the cameras, I had absolutely no experience catching air. I had caught maybe five feet of air and all of a sudden I'm catching a hundred feet of air forty feet high. I was totally out of control heading for a tree. I didn't actually black out; I just don't remember anything about it.

Kristen hit the base of the tree and got a bloody nose. She walked away a celebrity. At the time, she got what she wanted.

Arlo Eisenberg, a pioneer in the mid-1990s of so-called aggressive in-line skating, wanted to be different, too, but attention and risk were side effects rather than goals.

I didn't do things *because* they're dangerous. Being a young guy, you have a lot of energy and want some kind of athletic outlet. For me, and I think for a lot of people in our generation, football and baseball aren't the answer. For some reason, whatever factors went into it, there's an anti-establishment sentiment. We want to do things by our own rules, and we want to do things that are new and different that haven't been predetermined for us.

The Adrenaline Pump Most kids fulfill their need for a thrill by drag racing in their old Honda or experimenting with sex. Others, because of where they grow up or how their friends have fun, find themselves surfing big waves or skiing the backcountry. Chances are good that, if they feel competent enough that the thrill supersedes the fear, they go out for the rush repeatedly.

Getting an adrenaline rush is certainly one reason why athletes continue to go to extremes year after year. Does that mean they have an "adrenaline addiction"? Maybe some do, but it would be inaccurate to say that most of the adventurers, record holders, pioneers, and gold medalists in this book have an uncontrollable hunger for danger, a base desire for bad odds—that they're junkies, as in, "They can't stop themselves. They have an adrenaline addiction."

The Competence Rush The professional athlete's love of an adrenaline spike should almost never be linked to compulsive behavior or being out of control. Quite the opposite is true. It's more appropriate to say that taking a risk and succeeding because of their wits and skill feels orgasmic. As stunt biker T. J. Lavin says, "I'm more likely to get an adrenaline rush from something that gives me satisfaction than from something that makes me scared. When I know I'm going to nail a trick, and there is no fear, it's the greatest rush."

Pushing Physical Limits Many of these athletes also thrive on extreme physical challenge, like the recruits in boot camp who look at an obstacle course and yell, "Yahoo!" Rat Sult, street luge and snow mountain biking champion, puts it in personal terms: "The more pressure, the harder something is, the more I like it." They relish chances to test their fitness and sharpen their minds in outrageous circumstances.

This is the mentality of an adventure racer who treks 350 miles up rocks, into canyons, over white water, through the desert and mud, and across a vast lake for nine days and labels all that nonstop deprivation and strain "incredibly satisfying." A few weeks later, after my toenails grew back and the intestinal parasites died, I even started to call it "fun."

Self-Discovery For some, the allure of pushing past normal limits is in coming to grips with fears of the unknown and fostering the ability to handle change. World record skydiver Jim McCormick, a motivational speaker by profession, sums up the huge attraction of going to the edge for his audiences by saying "the greatest rewards in life go to the

CHAMPION ENDURANCE ATHLETE CHLOË LANTHIER-DAVID TRAINS IN WHISTLER, BRITISH COLUMBIA.

risk takers." Why? Because they learn to accept fear and move beyond their barriers and boundaries.

> I don't take risks just for the sake of taking risks. The reason I move out of my comfort zone on a regular basis is that I always learn more about myself in that setting. It gives me a tremendous amount of self-insight. It teaches me how I can respond to adversity, how I can do it better next time. It gives me lessons I can apply in my life.

Environmental Love Affairs These athletes love the environment where they play, and the harder they play, the more they are awakened to the wonders of that environment. It could be a city street, a 20,000-foot peak, or open ocean.

In the 1998 Raid Gauloise adventure race in Ecuador, teams stared at their maps in dread. They had to navigate to a checkpoint at the top of the volcano Cotopaxi in the Cordillera Central of the Andes in the north-central part of the country. At 5,897 meters—19,347 feet—it is the highest active volcano in the world. A cone-shaped mass, the top 3,000 feet have year-round snow cover, yet the volcano continuously emits clouds of steam from its lava-filled crater. Cotopaxi's slopes are covered with ash and rocks from eruptions. Ian Adamson, who has claimed world records as a kayaker and set precedents as an adventure racer, says this is a spot he will never forget.

> We struggled up Cotopaxi. There were only two teams* that made it. We were racing up this volcano—if you can call it racing at 20,000

---

*The other team was Cathy Sassin's, his former teammate and friend, who is also featured in this book.

feet—with everyone in full mountaineering gear. We had crampons and ice axes, we were roped in and all that sort of stuff. We were pulling our way up the hill and finally managed to make it to the top. Just being able to stand on the top of this smoking volcano, having climbed seven hours up icefalls and crevasses and seeing the clouds below us. Looking down onto the clouds, down onto the helicopter that was coming up with the film crew, we were thinking that, by itself, as a single moment in life it is amazing. Then you patch it together with the rest of the race, and the whole thing is indescribable. You can't explain the feeling of emotion and accomplishment that come along with it.

This is the avenue of the volcanoes. You can see all these other volcanoes poking up through the clouds. The clouds hang down at around 15,000 to 18,000 feet. So you look a couple thousand feet down on the clouds. You also look though blue ice—there's permanent snow and ice—and perfectly clear blue skies above. You can see forever in any direction. You can see there are little peaks poking above the clouds and little glimpses of the valley below when the clouds break through.

For the most part, the athletes not only love their playgrounds, they also honor them. They consciously connect their enjoyment of risk in their surroundings with respecting and being in touch with them. Scot Schmidt, a renowned extreme skier for more than two decades, admits: "The mountains are dangerous, especially if you go for the big stuff. The only thing that keeps me from being scared—I don't like being scared—is having a relationship with the mountain." In a belief that is congruent with Native American spiritualism, Scot tunes into the energy, or spirits, of the mountain.

Sherpas, the ethnic group most closely associated with Mount Everest, worship the mountain itself. Sherpa Jamling Tenzing Norgay, who summitted Everest in 1996:

WILL GADD ASCENDS THE ROCK, THEN MOVES TO THE ICE OVERHANG
ON A DIFFICULT MIXED ROUTE HE PUT UP IN VAIL, COLORADO. IT
IS RATED M9, WITH THE CURRENT DIFFICULTY LEVEL REACHING M10
FOR ONLY ONE ROUTE IN ICELAND, ALSO PUT UP BY WILL.

Everest is Mother Goddess of the world. Mountains are the places where the gods live. When we climb we climb with respect. We perform ceremonies to ask for safe passage on the mountain. The ceremonies are just between us and the gods.

Every time the Tsunami Rangers head out on a kayaking adventure, they stand on the beach and ask the ocean to "Let us pass or give a sign." They look for something like a sudden gust of wind, a huge wave that breaks hard, or a shark fin. Jim Kakuk doesn't consider this a ritual or a prayer, although there are Rangers who do. He calls it a "mind switch." It's a personal moment that helps him prepare to pass through the surf zone and enter the water planet—to be ready for a complete transition to the ocean and its rules.

This experience of "honoring the playground" does not just apply to nature, either. Louis Zamora, an in-line skating champion by the age of seventeen, has a sense of "making the most of what the streets have to offer" and appreciating them because they offer an opportunity for friendship and fun.

In their own way, all the athletes have a relationship with their world that is fundamental to their athletic success and the key to the sublime pleasure they get out of taking risks again and again.

Living with Passion While "competence rush" or "pushing physical limits" may describe why someone gravitates to a particular sport, there is a more general reason why many return to the edge year after year. They live with passion. If there is any aspect of their personalities and motivation that both binds them with people who are not extreme athletes and inspires anyone who comes in contact with them, it's this.

Big-wave surfer Jeff Clark describes these athletes very simply: "Their blood flows." They know it, they cherish the intensity of their lives, and they try to maintain it through injury, aging, and the demands of "normal" life like parenthood.

Alex Lowe,* the first man to climb many frozen waterfalls and unpronounceable peaks like Kwangde Nup in Nepal and Rakekniven in Antarctica, is the father of three boys. As is common for extreme athletes with children, some people chide him for taking risks. Alex keeps a particular story in mind that reminds him of the vital link between his passion for vertical adventures and his role as a parent.

I went over to Nepal and did a relatively difficult new route on a remote peak with my friend Steve, who had a son who was about five or six at the time. I asked him how he felt about being a father, and being there in Nepal, because I was having questions at that time. This was right after my first son, Max, was born in 1988. Steve said, when he was about twelve, he was walking downtown with his father. A friend of his father's that he hadn't seen in a long time came up to him and said to his dad—a conservative businessman who took care of the family and didn't do anything risky, except risk heart disease by not being active—"It's great to see you again! Are you still scuba diving?" Steve's father had never told him that he had ever scuba dived and his father's reaction was, "No, I haven't done anything like that since I had children." When Steve heard that, he had an immediate glow of admiration that his father had scuba dived, then when his father said, no, he hadn't done it since he had a family, he was devastated. He thought, here I am, the cause of my father not doing this. To him, that would have been the neatest thing that his father could have done.

As a father, Steve thought about that and decided to carry on, to share these experiences with his kids. Turn them on to things and teach them to be rational people who enjoy exciting situations in life. Make good judgments and enjoy risky activities in a positive way.

*On October 5, 1999, an avalanche on 26,291-foot Shishapangma in Chinese Tibet ended Alex Lowe's earthly life. Nevertheless, I respectfully refer to him in the present tense throughout this book.

That sums up my philosophy. I don't see myself being out of control in doing what I do in the first place. And I want to turn my kids on to the same pleasures I've experienced in pursuing things like that.

> **Inspiring passion in family and friends has more enduring value than just staying alive for them.**

Do These Athletes Have Anything in Common Other Than Risk Taking?

Extreme athletes wouldn't be able to sustain such intensity in their lives without a strong sense of personal responsibility. It doesn't matter if the athlete is seventeen or seventy, one element of character that binds them is that they tend not to point fingers. Right or wrong, they chose the line, paddled the boat, fixed the ropes, or picked the wave.

In January 1999, Shaun Palmer made a well-publicized attempt to take four gold medals in a single X Games. His dominance in snowboard racing was undisputed, but he faced other dominant forces in the free skiing, snow mountain biking, and snowmobile race events. All eyes were on him as he pushed hard in the early rounds of the skiercross event and won his first two heats. Then came the finals; he lost time coming out of the gate and never recovered. At the bottom of the hill as top finishers celebrated, the story of Shaun's slow start circulated. He had snagged a ski tip on a piece of torn Astroturf at the gate—a legitimate cause for protest. Shaun did not protest; he congratulated the winner. No blame. No excuses.

How Can They Do These Things and Not Kill Themselves?

The companion question to "why" athletes do these extreme things is, of course, "how." Will Gadd, a great multisport extreme athlete, starts down the road to answering it by noting: "Extreme sports improve situational awareness. By doing them again and again, you get better at choosing when to draw back and when to push forward."

The following chapters get more specific with how-to information about visualization, tactical decision making, sport-specific training, injury prevention, and so on. Much of it is information that can make you better at whatever you do, whether it's on the edge or far from it.

STEPH DAVIS CLIMBS THE LINE SHE NAMED INSHALLAH ("GOD WILLING" IN URDU) ON SHIPTON SPIRE IN PAKISTAN. THERE, IN SHARP CONTRAST TO HER EXPERIENCE IN FITZROY, "EVERYTHING JUST KEPT WORKING."

STORMING FITZROY

Patagonia eats climbers. Swept by strong winds called pamperos and hit by ferocious weather, particularly at higher elevations in the Andean foothills, it treats no one kindly.

Knowing full well that "you can be killed if you're on a peak and there's a storm," Steph Davis went there in 1997 to attempt a new route on a rock formation called Fitzroy with her friend Charlie Fowler. Both climbers have great credentials, but Steph's youth, gender, and versatility make her one of a kind. She flashes extraordinary skills on hard cracks, long rock routes in the mountains, walls, boulders, high-altitude routes—whatever nature has carved out or pushed upward. The big granite mountain they chose is named after an explorer who, ironically, had a reputation for being adverse to change. For one thing, he interpreted the Bible literally, which is why he had such contentious discussions with the naturalist on his Patagonia expedition—Charles Darwin.

Steph and Charlie could have timed the trip better: they arrived on December 8, 1996, shortly *after* ten consecutive days of near perfect weather. For the next two and a half months, they rode out storms. "We were always waiting for the weather, then climbing and praying that nothing happened during the climb because it changes so fast."

From December 8 to February 25, they saw one day of good weather.

They started to go stir-crazy, so they tackled a few free climbs smaller and easier than their target despite the bad conditions. Among them were repeats of three excellent routes, the North Tower in Chile, the Ruby y Azur on the formation called Media Luna, and the Pialoa on El Mocho—all about 2,000 feet. Unlike Fitzroy, which is also about 2,000 feet but requires a

5,000-foot climb to get to its base, the others start low so they are sheltered from the really foul weather. From the glacier to the top and back takes about a day, whereas Fitzroy takes almost three days in decent weather. And their hearts were set on a new route on Fitzroy.

They eventually went up a couloir, or steep gully, on the west side of Fitzroy, which had not been done before. They calculated that they could ascend in less than perfect weather because of the mixed nature of the climbing there, that is, sections of bare rock were interspersed with snow- and ice-covered terrain. Knowing they will be on snow and ice, the climbers on a mixed route are equipped with crampons and ice tools; patches of icy rock pose no particular problem.

In unpleasant, but not horrible conditions, they got up fairly high to the shoulder of Fitzroy. Having successfully made a new approach to about 5,000 feet, they hoped to speed to the summit on an existing route—the American Route—which would require 2,000 feet of rock climbing. On the rock face, they would be wearing shoes designed to stick to dry rock and would ascend barehanded to grab flakes and cracks. A storm would fill the cracks in the rock with ice, making it slippery. It would also make it nearly impossible for them to insert their hardware into the rock because ice would be where the gear should go.

Then the storm hit.

They had to dig a snow cave at the base of the rock because of fierce winds, snow, sleet, and soft hail. In Patagonia, these winds have enough force to blow climbers off rock. As they dug, more snow would fill the cave. It never got better. They got snowed into the cave and ran out of food. Their only choice was to descend in the storm.

> We had to go down some ice slopes. It was the kind of ice that wasn't hard enough to put an ice screw in, or to make a thread [two ways you can rappel down ice]. So we chopped out some bollards; you chop with your ice axes and carve a big round blob on the face of the ice. Then you lay your ropes around it and rappel down. The last bollard was huge and in-cut—so big that we even joked about what a great bollard it was. Charlie went down first off it in this really bad storm. I closed my eyes against the sleet and when I opened them, the ropes were gone.

There were thousands of feet of air below us because we were descending a huge serac—an ice cliff—that dropped down far below to a gulley full of snow. If we fell off the sheer edge of the serac, we'd free-fall into that couloir. I thought that's what happened to Charlie. I was sure he was dead or far away, and I didn't have any ropes anyway, so I didn't know what I could do for him, but I knew I was screwed, too. I yelled into the wind, but it was pointless. So I started downclimbing on the ice—kicking into it with my crampons one foot at a time, hitting with my ice axes one hand at a time. I figured I had a slim chance of getting down the route alone.

Eventually, amazingly, Charlie started climbing up and met me with the ropes dragging behind him. He said, "The ropes blew off the bollard. I knew what you'd be thinking and I knew I had to get up here as fast as I could."

As it turned out, Steph never would have made it downclimbing because, even on the easy snow slopes below, the wind was blowing so hard it repeatedly knocked both of them down. They had to belay each other, crawling, on places where they'd walked before and did multiple rappels where downclimbing wasn't feasible.

It took them twelve hours of fighting to get down, just as it had taken twelve hours of fighting to get up. Normally, the climb down takes a quarter of the time it takes to ascend.

At the time I didn't have any fear about it. A trip like that is so physically and mentally taxing, with so many emotional ups and downs, that I was numb by that point. You always have to be excited about climbing and be prepared to go for it; at the same time you're always waiting, trying to be patient because you're not getting the weather. I was just dealing with what we had to do, which is strange because usually that would be a horrifying situation.

Instead of having a lot of fear, I was thinking, "Charlie's dead. I have no ropes. All right, then." Sometimes in a really big crisis you feel that way—just dead calm. I figured I was either going to die or not. The alternatives were very clear.

Steph and Charlie allowed themselves one day of recovery, then repeated their approach route and returned to their snow cave. The following day, February 18, they started toward the summit of Fitzroy on the American Route. Snow and ice choked the route and slowed their pace. A little more than halfway up—about a thousand feet from the summit—weather forced them to descend to their bivy (bivouac) on the glacier.

Steph's conclusion: "Reaching the summit is always a goal, but the biggest victory is living to try again."

Learn the exercises that develop visualizing, centering, and other key skills that train the body and mind to work together. In many situations, it is critical to have several minds and bodies working together, too. You will discover how world champion teams achieve that.

PICABO Street never actually skied the hill in Nagano that led to her Olympic gold medal in Super G until the event. Other competitors knew the race hill in their guts; she knew it only in her mind.

Everyone else I raced against had skied it at least six times. I had never skied it. I had rolled my right ankle and got a two-and-a-half-degree tear in my ankle two days before the Super G in Nagano. We didn't tell anyone, but it's the reason why I didn't preski on the race hill.

I had ridden down the hill the year before on my coach's back while recovering from knee surgery. Not at high speed—we had just slipped

down and checked out the terrain—so I could visualize it to some degree. And after I inspected it in the morning, from the time I inspected it to the time I ran it, I must have run that course a million times in my head. I couldn't visualize it to the umpteenth degree as if I'd physically run it, but I did visualize it. I couldn't get a whole sensation—the feeling in my belly—but that was fine. I could visualize myself doing it and ending up here and there.

Techniques like visualization and centering have long been in the repertoire of champions. A lot of them have arrived at the techniques by chance—maybe they have a ritual or superstition that makes them feel ready—but there are many ways to learn these techniques as part of the path to getting into the proverbial Zone.

A Champion's Program for Mind-Body Connection

Figure skater Brian Boitano isn't an extreme athlete per se, but his training program to perfect these techniques is straightforward as well as tried-and-true: his gold medal performance in the 1988 Olympics in Calgary was a spectacular display of the level of body-mind connection that is vital in extreme sports.

Brian went to a coach who taught him exercises to put the "inner body" on the same agenda as the "outer body." In professional athletics, he's a trailblazer when it comes to this. He actually created an entire conditioning program for the nonphysical part of himself so he would win a gold medal at the Olympics. Based on how many great athletes in extreme sports talk openly about the importance of "positive energy" and "feeling centered," for example, it is clear that Brian's approach to peak performance is consistent with theirs.

> **The whole athlete has to be prepared to go to the edge, not just the body.**

When he was eighteen years old, Brian began working with Joyah French, a performance coach whom he called his "secret weapon." By the time he was twenty-four and heading for Calgary for the 1988 Olympics, Brian was adept at using four techniques that many extreme athletes have now adopted to some degree:

1. Physical exercises to prepare the brain and nervous system for optimal performance;
2. Visualization, which may be described as "sensualization" when multiple senses are involved;
3. Quick relaxation; and
4. Silencing the negative ego. The negative ego is that fear-based creature inside that whines, "This is really hard. I don't think you're good enough to do it."

Exercises to Prepare the Brain and Nervous System for Optimal Performance Start with cross crawls, which you'll want to do before a practice as well as before an event. Stand with your feet shoulder width apart. Lift your left knee up to waist level by bending your leg at the knee, and then touch it with your right elbow. Place the left foot back on the floor as you lift up your right knee and touch with your left elbow. Repeat this for one minute, either while standing in one place or while you walk. Keep your head forward.

The action has multiple positive effects. It improves left-to-right eye movement and binocular vision. It forces blood into the frontal lobe of the brain so you think more clearly. In Joyah's terms, "It balances the hemispheres, so it improves coordination, brings your energy up if you're tired and down if you're hyperactive."

Today, many professional athletes, particularly those who rely on their timing and balance for success, consider the move a routine part of their pre-event preparation. When Joyah introduced Brian to it in the early 1980s, though, almost no one did it and he resisted. He didn't want to look ridiculous as the cameras followed him around backstage. Joyah says he changed his mind in a hurry: "It produced such quick results for him that he immediately started to trust it."

Professional athletes aren't the only ones who use exercises like cross crawls, lazy 8s, hook-ups, and other physical activities that prepare the brain and entire nervous system for optimal performance. Kids in progressive schools in Canada and the United States are doing them in a program called Brain Gym, devised by Dr. Paul Dennison, head of California's Educational Kinesiology Foundation. The result of decades of research, he based Brain Gym on the belief that the left and right hemispheres of the brain do not always function in conjunction with each other and certain exercises or movements help to connect them. He's found that the exercises are particularly useful in times of stress or when learning blocks occur.*

To do lazy 8s, stand up and raise your arm in front of you at shoulder height. While tracing a figure-8 with your finger, follow your finger with your eyes. Do it for a minute. This exercise is designed to help you focus and concentrate.

Hook-ups could help you focus and balance your mental and physical energy. Cross your legs Indian style as well as your arms in a comfortable way that automatically induces calm.

*For more details, visit the Educational Kinesiology Foundation Web site, www.braingym.org.

Two-Part Visualization A number of purely mind exercises also prepare the extreme athlete for top performance. As Picabo Street's story early in the chapter vividly illustrates, visualization is a fundamental part of a champion's repertoire. Brian used a two-part visualization technique that led to a classic story about his win at the 1988 Olympics in Calgary:

> "The Star-Spangled Banner" was playing and I said to myself, "This tempo is too fast." My nightly visualizations for about a year had been complete up until that moment—*exactly* as I'd visualized everything. The jumping, the way the audience responded, the way I responded to the audience. First I did this, then I cried, then I laughed—all that was visualized. When it happened, it was like I was dreaming. It was surreal to me. Then I got up to the podium after winning the gold medal and the National Anthem started playing and I thought, "This isn't 'The Star-Spangled Banner' that I imagined. It's too fast!" I imagined "The Star-Spangled Banner" going, "Daaah, daaah, daaah, daaah, daaah, dah," but it started differently. The drums came in and it was "dah, dah, dah, dah, dah, dah," and I thought, "This is not real! The tempo's wrong!" That's what made me realize it *was* real.

To begin the two-part visualization technique, first visualize a place where you feel fabulous. It doesn't have to be an actual spot on the planet. The visualization can involve sensations of sunshine and a chill in the air, or maybe it's just a bubble of white light.

Second, within that environment, see yourself going through each move. You might close your eyes and see yourself teeing off, or delivering a speech, or preparing dinner in a very organized fashion. The important thing is that all you see is your body in that ideal place performing perfectly again and again. If your activity is too fast to visualize, imagine the perfect beginning and ending, the perfect takeoff and landing.

> When a trick is too fast to visualize in
> detail, visualize the clean start and finish.
> Your body will handle the rest.

Brian did something unique to ensure this performance-related visualization was consistent. He told Joyah everything he wanted to do, feel, see, and hear during his program, then she created audiotapes based on his descriptions. Over and over again, he would listen to the sound of her voice describing his actions so he absorbed the flow of his perfect routine in his deepest consciousness. Adding an auditory element to the visualization exercise engages one more sense in the process and may even help to activate other senses.

The two-part visualization technique has obvious benefits for athletes such as freestyle bikers, skateboarders, in-line skaters, sky-surfers, and others who do "tricks." Air in the West looks like air in the East. A skysurfer can visualize her ideal space and call it "Florida" if that's where the competition is.

It's enormously useful for athletes who don't do tricks as well, though. The athlete can visualize being clear-minded, centered, and breathing easily, and can see outcomes—no injuries, top performance, feeling proud and full of energy. All of those are what Joyah calls "mind-mending aspects" of the activity and can be visualized beforehand. For example, a free climber can't know every move because the specific challenges of the wall are unknown. So the exercise is to visualize balance, the ecstasy of powering past an overhang, the flow of the climb, a feeling of coordination. A kayaker can visualize the wave coming and the timing of the paddle slicing into it. It doesn't matter what wave or where. It's a way to get the body in touch with the rhythm of that environment.

STEPH DAVIS CAN VISUALIZE THE BALANCE AND COORDINATION SHE
NEEDS TO DO A CHALLENGING 5.12 ROUTE LIKE THIS ONE, CALLED
BROKEN BRAIN, OUTSIDE MOAB, UTAH.

Big-wave surfer Jeff Clark does an exercise that supports this kind of visualization: "I'm a freak for studying waves, even a trivial, little wave. I'll watch it and mind-surf it." He imagines paddling cleanly through the cold water at maximum speed, and having perfect timing as the wave lifts him. He sees himself going backward up a giant wave as it's building—paddling forward at maximum speed, but watching the wave draw him up as if he's not paddling at all. He feels himself breaking free of its force pulling up and over. At that point, the wave is vertical and he snaps to his feet and guides his surfboard down the contours of the face of this wave as it's jacking up and hurling behind him. He feels the contours and bumps of the wave as he guides his board through. In his mind, he tastes the salt water, feels the rush, hears the breaking wave.

> **Visualization not only locks the experience in the brain so the body's performance is more automatic, but it also stimulates sensations of success.**

Sensualization Anna Wise, a renowned biofeedback and brain wave training expert, coined the term "sensualization" to describe the kind of multisensory visualization that Jeff creates and that Brian relied on to "hear" the orchestra play "The Star-Spangled Banner" as he prepared to get on the ice at Calgary. It's the kind of experience that Picabo strives for—"a whole sensation—the feeling in my belly." It doesn't necessarily come naturally. In her book *The High-Performance Mind,* Anna recommends doing exercises focused on each sense to develop the ability. She says, "The stronger the image you can evoke, using as many of your senses as possible, the more successful will be your outcome."*

*Anna Wise, *The High Performance Mind* (Jeremy P. Tarcher/Putnam, 1997), p. 96.

To create a sensualization customized to your activity, follow these steps. To clarify how to do the exercise, Anna speculates how an athlete faced with Picabo's situation in Nagano could apply the steps to arrive at a multisensory image.

1. Identify your access sense.

Everyone has an access sense. It is the strongest sense you have when you close your eyes. In some people, the access sense is much stronger than other senses. For example, if your access sense is vision, you may be able to close your eyes and see intense colors and sharp images, but can't imagine how a fish smells. Some people have a similarity in the strength and depth of their senses, so it's harder for them to determine what the access sense is.

Some people get frustrated trying to model their sports heroes or others who talk about the value of visualization. They appreciate its value and keep trying to do it, but their access sense is not visual, so basically they *can't* visualize. Give them an image and they think, "I don't see it. I just can't do this." There may be athletes who intellectually know that the visualization process is a valuable tool to improve, but they can't visualize because their access sense is touch or smell. Very likely, they give up trying. If you find your access sense, you can either build toward visualization, or just use another sense to do the same thing that Picabo did with visualization in Nagano.

To determine your access sense, get into a relaxed position, close your eyes, and discover what your mind does when you ask it to imagine certain things. For example, to test your visual sense, start by imagining as many colors as possible, including black and white. Watch clouds moving across a windy sky, light a match in a dark room, and so on. Think of at least a half dozen images that are just as specific. Do the same with the other senses: touch (the soft fur of a kitten), hearing (the howl of a police siren), smell (freshly brewed coffee), taste (minty toothpaste), and experience, or kinesthesia (walking barefoot on wet sand). Anna recommends tape-recording the suggestions ahead of time, so you are merely responding to the suggestions during the exercise and not thinking through ideas.

Rate the outcome to find your access sense. If one type of sensation you imagined was extremely lifelike, more vivid and distinctive than others even for a moment, then you have probably found your access sense. Even if nothing seemed that realistic, think about how you would rank the strongest sensations—clear, hazy, dim—in order to determine your access sense.

2. Use your access sense to put yourself into the experience you want to sensualize.

Picabo did this by seeing the slope, seeing every turn and nuance of the course. A kinesthetic person might feel the bumps on the hill. A tactile person could start with a sensation of chill on her cheeks.

3. Run through your senses randomly and see what *else* is available, that is, what sensations you can imagine to some degree, even if they aren't as strong as the access sense—tactile (skin and touch), kinesthetic (body), smell, taste, hearing, sight. Do this by asking yourself questions about the entire experience:

> Can you feel the wind on your skin?
> Is it sunny or overcast?
> Do you feel stinging cold, or is the temperature mild?
> What do your goggles feel like?
> Are you grasping the poles firmly or lightly?
> Do you feel the poles planting in the snow?
> How far apart are your legs?
> Do you feel the bend in your knees?

What does your lip protection taste like?

Do your lips feel smooth or rough?

Do your clothes smell like the wood burning in the fireplace back at
the lodge?

Do you hear a teammate cheering for you as you leave the gate?

Is there music?

Because Picabo knows the sensation of skiing so well, in all likelihood her mind is able to translate what a mogul looks like to what it feels like. Anna believes it is also possible, however, for people to go through a series of detailed questions like this for an activity they have never done and vividly imagine it. (We've probably all heard someone come away from a first experience saying, "It's just as I imagined it.")

4. Now run through your senses logically. Go back to the image you created with your access sense and add sensations, one at a time. That is, keep going over and over the experience adding just one more sensation each time until you've tried to add every kind of sensation.

By injecting so much detail into the imagery, you may arrive at an experience that will not be identical to the competition or other activity. But that can be extremely useful, too, as long as the sensations convey positive feelings and not emotional baggage like performance anxiety. As stated earlier, the point of an exercise like this is not only to lock the experience in the brain so the body's performance is more automatic, but also to stimulate any sensation of success. Integrate any sensation you've had when you've been at your peak.

Extreme athletes have a distinct reason to visualize, or sensualize, other than winning a competition. For them, peak performance often includes managing life-threatening situations, so strong imagery of how to handle a problem can turn a crisis into a routine occurrence. Steve Verner, the camera-flyer half of the Double Trouble skysurfing team, made a practice of analyzing what could go wrong on a skydive and thinking through the problem. Then he turned it into a series of visualizations that he regularly uses to keep himself current on emergency procedures.

Skydivers have a lot to deal with—in-flight awareness, proper deployment of the canopy, and flying and landing each involve dozens of variables. Camera-flyers' safety issues go far beyond those of regular skydivers, especially when they fly with skysurfers. They fly in close proximity to a board that's whipping around at high speed. They are expected to grip that board at times—a move that clipped the lens off one camera-flyer's helmet-mounted equipment and it could have removed his head. They also have other issues related to their suits with "wings" attached at the wrist and waist that give them some ability to adjust how fast they fall. Finally, there is the simple danger of shooting video in the air. The camera represents ten pounds on the head and comes with gear around the face, like a ring sight that restricts vision. And altitude awareness is a problem for the camera-flyer, who is shooting video and not glancing at the ground or at an altimeter. In short, many things could go wrong.

Steve's habit of mentally acting out the possible problems has already saved him once—or at least given him peace of mind—during a serious canopy malfunction. He knew precisely what to do and remained calm. Everything took place in a couple of seconds.

How Visualization, or Sensualization, Helps

Aerobatics

U.S. Navy Blue Angel Mark Dunleavy: "In the preshow briefing demo pilots have eyes closed, visualizing as the boss is giving the calls; sometimes you'll see them move their hands for the controls of the aircraft in a way that's appropriate for the maneuver being executed. They'll actually 'fly' the entire demonstration in the brief."

Kayaking—Freestyle

Jamie Simon: Jamie made a trip to New Zealand a year ahead of the December 1999 world competition to see the spot in the river where the event would occur and to memorize its features. Before she left she explained, "I will spend the next year visualizing that spot."

Kayaking—Surf Zones, Rock Gardens, and Sea Caves

Jim Kakuk: "Visualization is one of the tools the Tsunami Rangers use in preparing to escalate our level of challenge."

Mountainbike Racing

Pistol Pete Loncarevich: "There might be seventy-five different turns—I want to remember every single root and rock that's on that course. Visualization plays a big role in building your confidence and helping you overcome fears that you have."

Skiing

Kristen Ulmer (on her historic descent of Grand Teton): "I got to the top and I was terrified. The conditions were awful. The risk was very high, but I wanted to do it and I saw that it could be possible. I visualized it happening entirely from experience—not stupidity or blind faith. Then I realized, 'I can do this and not die.' The second I visualized it, I just turned my emotions off. Then off I went."

Skydiving

Dan Brodsky-Chenfeld (on one habit of his world championship skydiving team): "We all visualize on the way to altitude. That's part of the training, just like running in the morning. We do twelve jumps in a day—that's only twelve minutes of skydiving, but if you visualize every time you go to altitude, that's another two hours. The benefits of visualization are no secret. Any athlete, especially in a sport that only lasts minutes at a time, has no choice but to visualize."

You might find it useful to think of a fifth step in the sensual-ization process—planting the image deep in your mind. It is critical to take the multisensory image into the depths of the subconscious so it has the greatest effect. For most people, it's probably safe to say that this does not come naturally. This is why Brian Boitano's audiotape strategy is a great idea and why the next two elements of his pro-gram—relaxation and silencing the negative ego—help to ensure that the visualization really works.

Using Anna Wise's nomenclature, the practice of sensualizing described above utilizes alpha brain waves, but planting the imagery deep means involving low-frequency theta waves and even lower-fre-quency delta waves—those associated with intuition, among other things. According to Anna, it also means eliminating the chatter associ-ated with beta waves:

> One of the important characteristics of the brain wave pattern in peak performance is that it is not impeded with the daily chatter that people experience in their normal thought process. You don't want to be inhibited by worry, anxiety, list making, judging, self-critique, critique of others—any of what the yogis call the "squirming of the worm in the brain" or the "chattering of a thousand monkeys."

Essentially, in order to make visualization work for you when you face tense moments, learn how to calm down.

Quick Relaxation Relaxation exercises take many forms. Brian's imagined he was in an elevator, going from the tenth to the first floor. By the time he got very good at using the technique, he could get to the first floor in five seconds. Many athletes, notably Olympic gold medalist skiers Franz Klammer and Hermann Maier, are known for making jokes at the start, then taking only seconds to compose themselves with this kind of incredible mental discipline.

Brian's goal was "to relax myself to the point where I'm almost asleep. That means that I can allow myself to have the timing I need." Relaxation on that level means eliminating the jitters that randomly expend precious energy. It means getting ready to enter the Zone, that "experience of absolute effortlessness."* The legendary speed skier Franz Weber also aimed for a near-sleep relaxation. Eventually, he exceeded his expectations.

At a 1980 downhill competition in Aspen, Colorado, Franz was winning all the training runs by a second or two. After that, he went back to his room, closed his eyes, and calmly visualized all the turns and how he would handle them. He saw himself as absolute perfection, running the course over and over again in his mind. It was sunny that day in Aspen, and when he later got to the top of the mountain on the lift, he lay down on a warm concrete platform. He thought, "I have another twenty minutes to go before the race starts and I don't want to stand around at the start where there's a lot of talking and screaming." So he lay there, relaxed from head to toe—so relaxed that he fell asleep and missed the first qualifying run. He still made it in the second run.

> Once, I actually slipped out of the lift. I had asked another guy, "Please wake me up when I get to the top so I know when to lift my ski tips." There are about 100 yards where the lift is very low. He didn't wake me up and I slipped out of the chair. I was fine. I ended up winning the downhill.

Have a strategy to avoid being nervous.

---

*John Douillard, *Body, Mind and Sport* (Three Rivers Press, 1994), p. 4.

Additional Techniques for Quick Relaxation

Kayaker Jamie Simon makes a horse sound with her mouth. A certified massage therapist, Jamie finds that it relaxes all the muscles in her face: "I think if you're relaxed in your face, you can relax all over." Research supports her; studies have shown that facial muscles control the degree of tension in the entire body.*

Another tip from Jamie is to give the excess adrenaline a shape: "Close your eyes and picture all of your bones—your entire skeletal system. Get all that energy out of your soft tissue and into your skeletal system. I even picture my bones moving. I open my eyes and all the adrenaline is still there, but now it has form. My skin isn't so tingly that I can't perform. The adrenaline is there, but it's in a stable form. It's totally a mind game."

Biker Pistol Pete Loncarevich, surfer Jeff Clark, and ice climber Kim Csizmazia all use yoga breathing techniques to pull themselves together. Kim practices breathing deeply through her nose.

Pistol Pete also draws on his extensive training in Brazilian jujitsu to help him stay relaxed and centered. The breathing exercises, meditation, and other practices used in martial arts training all help the athlete quiet the mind and focus the senses. Several top athletes credit martial arts discipline with helping them relax on cue.

Luger Michael Shannon used to tense up at the start line every time. He couldn't breathe. On a daily basis, he started meditating. (This can be something as simple as thinking of one thing, like a number or an image, for minutes at a time.) He doesn't blow his starts anymore because he can quickly reclaim that calm he feels in meditation.

*Stephen Rae, "The Mental Game," *Men's Journal,* March 1999, p. 85.

JAMIE SIMON GOES VERTICAL TO PLAY IN THE HYDRAULIC. IN COM-
PETITION, SHE'LL STAY IN "THE HOLE" AS LONG AS POSSIBLE.
SHE CAN'T WASTE ENERGY ON NERVOUSNESS.

Silencing the Negative Ego The final technique in the program is silencing the negative ego. Some people don't seem to have one, do they? They blast through life without the burden of any part of their psyche telling them they are unworthy. At least they appear to do that. Perhaps at an early age, they discovered this exercise.

Identify the characteristics of your negative ego, the part of you that spews limiting, self-sabotaging, degrading, and defeating messages.

◆◆◆ What are the words your negative ego uses? Listen to that voice. The negative ego is the part of you that's afraid and needy. This is the doubter inside you that assumes you're going to fail, and "fail" can mean a lot of things—lose, get hurt, back off, back down, slow down. Joyah French counsels: "The last rung of the ladder toward success and freedom is doubt."

◆◆◆ Give the doubter a name. Talk with it. Call it something innocuous like Garfield or Elmer Fudd that doesn't convey power or a booming voice.

Once you isolate your negative ego and get some perspective on it, you can manage it. It's a giant step toward tuning in more clearly to the part of you that enjoys and expects success.

> **If you question your ability, you only have a slight chance of succeeding.**

> ## Guidelines to Coordinate the Inner Body and the Outer Body
>
> Practice these exercises before training and events. They only take a few minutes.
>
> ••• Physical exercises like cross crawls to boost brain and nervous system performance;
> ••• Visualization involving as many senses as possible;
> ••• A relaxation technique that calms you down quickly; and
> ••• Silencing the part of you that doubts your ability to succeed.

Program for a Winning Team

Many extreme sports are called solo activities, but in reality not many of them are completely. And, in some activities—free climbing, high-altitude mountaineering, skydiving, glacier trekking, and white-water boating, to name just a few—absorption with individual achievement undermines the chances of success and amplifies the danger for everyone. Teamwork becomes a survival mechanism, not a fuzzy concept. Take self-focused people with a mixed bag of agendas to Everest and some of them will probably not come back.

If you need to coordinate the efforts of a group, whether it's a kids' soccer team, a software-development team, or six adventure racers, consider following the advice of some of the best extreme sports teams in the world.

Arizona Airspeed is a skydiving team composed of four men, two of whom were "leaders" of highly ranked rival teams—neither of which had won a world championship. In coming together in 1994 for the express purpose of winning the gold medal at the world meet, they realized that two "leaders" on one team was not a good idea. They called in Dr. Bob Moore, an organizational and sports psychologist whose practice centers on "building team systems in order to achieve world-class results."

Eliminating defensiveness in conversation Bob hoped they could achieve certain outcomes, like decision making by consensus, but he knew a procedure like that couldn't be dictated. It needed to emerge as a normal and logical part of their team experience. Taking steps to eliminate defensiveness in communication was a better starting point. Bob wanted them to see their differences of opinion as vital energy for problem-solving and decision-making dialogue—all very nice except that many people are selective about when and to whom they'll listen. Bob says this is very common with groups of all-male athletes particularly: "I've worked in situations where a team member wouldn't take feedback from any other team member, just a specific person. There were politics in the communication."

Dan Brodsky-Chenfeld, one of the "leaders," said that one exercise that helped them get to that level of communication was a "pass the rock meeting."

> It's a scheduled time every week where you can say anything you like, first going with something positive. Whoever has the rock is the only one allowed to speak—everyone else must listen. Even if you think it's a dumb thing, you have to bring it up. Sure, sometimes, it's more like pass the bat or pass the gun.

Consensus Decision Making From achieving lack of defensiveness in their communication, they moved smoothly to consensus decision making. Robert Nagle, of Team Eco-Internet—adventure racing's equivalent of Arizona Airspeed—believes their ability to make important decisions by consensus is one of his team's fundamental strengths. Specifically, it's helped them pull off navigational magic in the wilderness. And Todd Skinner emphasizes that, in planning a free climb, the last thing you and your buddies want is to "climb the wall for 2,000 feet, then have the wall go completely blank." Everyone has to feel that, no matter what happens, they all agreed on the line: "We argue over it, draw it, show each other where we think the other is wrong. Then we come up with a conclusion about how to go."

Procedures to Fix Problems Bob also wanted every member of Airspeed to buy into a system of procedures. An important one is the debrief structure after a skydive. First, an individual would say something positive about his performance, then state what he could do better. After that, other teammates could critique him *with* suggestions on how to fix the glitch. Dan notes that no one assumes he had fifty seconds of greatness—forty is good—"so it's okay to focus on the ten seconds of crap." And even if someone feels like his performance in the skydive was so embarrassing it was like being naked in church, he should find something in it that felt good, like flying away from it at high speed after the formation attempts were over.

> It's not that you hide from the things that need to be fixed by using this approach, it's just you have a much more positive presence. It's much more fun and people stay more enthusiastic. The rule is that you are not allowed to be defensive in this process. You only give a critique if you can honestly evaluate what you've seen and evaluated what your thoughts are before you speak.

Shared Leadership Another potential hurdle was leadership. Dan and Jack Jeffries, who actually had taken the initiative to put the "dream team" together, were both "leaders." This is not to say that their partners, Mark Kirkby and Kirk Verner, were inherently not. In a traditional military or sports team structure, however, there is only one captain. Bob firmly believes this model is woefully inadequate in extreme sports, businesses, and a lot of other environments.

> The downside of an authoritarian arrangement is that once that person is outside his or her limits in terms of perspective, ability, skill, then the system is stuck because the team is still following the leader. There's no way to bring out all of the best energy.

The team worked toward and achieved a shared leadership approach. One element of the evolution is a continuous improvement process, which is also a way of neutralizing conflict potential. Bob collected everyone's ideas about how to do things better. The team tried them all and plotted the results on a spreadsheet. It was an illustration that everyone had something substantial to contribute to improving performance. Bob says this exercise definitely "helped feed the system of nondefensive communication" that underlies so many of the other positive outcomes.

The role of the extended team of families, support personnel, and the fifth flyer, the camera person, in strengthening Airspeed is not incidental, either. Bob thinks of the team as "concentric circles of caring and support."

Guidelines for Building a Winning Team

- ◆◆◆ Make important decisions by consensus.
- ◆◆◆ Share leadership. Don't emulate the military.
- ◆◆◆ Set specific goals and regularly measure progress. Are goals being met or exceeded?
- ◆◆◆ Promote continuous improvement through all procedures—procedures that were designed by consensus.
- ◆◆◆ Resolve conflicts as quickly and fully as possible.
- ◆◆◆ Use mistakes as opportunities for learning and not for ridicule.

> ••• Live by values of honesty, respect, loyalty, inclusion, and equal-
> ity, and share your passion for making your dream of success a
> reality.

There is a final outcome that Bob believes is vital. It should be a natural outgrowth of the other elements of communication and leadership, but it isn't always. Adventure racer Cathy Sassin calls it "competitive teamwork," and Bob describes it this way:

> Get rid of any detrimental competition within the team and focus on the competition all being outside. If you can really achieve that and get the team to achieve that and work their competitive issues in a positive way, it's dynamite—highly charged, good collective energy.

Practically speaking, it means that water is team water, food is team food, and everyone should be expending the same amount of effort to achieve a common goal. It means a stronger biker giving a fatigued teammate help up the hill by giving a push or taking some weight, instead of just being patient with his pace. It belies the commonly held belief that "you're as weak as your weakest member" and replaces it with a concept of using everyone's strength to bring the weak person up to a higher performance level. The real-life application of this philosophy has had dramatic results for Cathy (see "Lessons in Action: Racing in Sundance Land").

Bob believes Cathy's "competitive teamwork" concept is valuable for teams that aim to succeed—whether that means being the first to arrive, reaching the top, throwing the best tricks, or doing something no group has ever done before.

> It's one of those systems, and energies, that has to be present for the team to realize its full potential. The sharing of resources—food,

information, whatever it is—being fully open to that is about commitment and commitment to team.

Every single team that manifests what we call high performance—not just a high-functioning team, but really, really high performance—has that kind of caring about each other going on. That ends up being a key variable. It can sound corny, but people end up loving each other. It's what happens. Some people get repelled by that idea, but it's really what works.

Even athletes in individual performance sports who have teammates—that is, they share a main sponsor or are part of something like the U.S. Ski Team—talk about this genuine caring as vital to their performance and their enjoyment of their sport.

> ### If you're on a team only to win, winning will disappoint you. Friendship supersedes winning.

Rollerblader Louis Zamora started skating for the team of his dreams when he was in his mid-teens. At seventeen, he said, "These were people I looked up to and now they're my best friends." He thinks they bring each other's performance levels up through "fun and friendship" more than just going out and practicing tricks.

And to add to the story about Picabo Street's Super G success in Nagano, she makes it clear that visualization and her personal performance were not the only vital elements at play that day:

Just before my run my service man, Cookie [Mike Kairys], was holding the radio out over the back of my head while my poles were

TEAM EXTREME WAS THE LAST TEAM TO CANOE TO THE FINISH POINT OF
THE 1995 ECO-CHALLENGE. MOST NEVER MADE IT NEAR THE FINISH, SO
THEIRS WAS A BIG VICTORY OF TEAMWORK AS WELL AS FITNESS.

over the wand. I was listening to music, I was stretching out, I was staying calm. I was enjoying being at the start with my teammate Clarkie [Kirsten Clark].

She ran up there and I was enjoying having her there. . . . To be perfectly honest, one of the most moving things for me was hearing her cheer for me when I left the start. I just wanted to wave and say, "Thank you." It made such a huge difference.

I'm used to Cookie and I love him to death. He's my man. He's 50 percent of my program. He makes my skis fast and I make them go. We're a team that way. He yells as long as he thinks I can hear him and I can hear him all the time. But when you have a teammate cheering for you, it's really something else. It made a huge difference and I've thanked her several times for it. I just hope I can return the favor some day.

RACING IN SUNDANCE LAND

Teams of five lined up behind each other like neat rows of soldiers that predawn morning. When a team got to the front, wranglers gave them three horses and sent them to a holding area. By the time *Good Morning America* arrived for a live feed, 159 people had reins in hand and another 106 were ready to run on the rock and dust alongside them. At the sound of the gun, the inaugural Eco-Challenge began. Competitors had, at most, ten days to complete the course of canyons, desert, rapids, and still water. No one except the race organizers knew exactly how long it was nor the extremes of temperature, elevation, dry and wet that lay ahead. Racers would discover their course as they moved from checkpoint to checkpoint, periodically picking up segments of maps.

For the teams that finished, the reward was 376 miles of spectacular Utah wilderness imbued with the soul of the Anasazi, the Navajo, and the Ute and the wild spirit of pioneers, cowboys, and misfits. Most teams would not claim that reward, though.

There were good reasons why most teams would never make it to the end of this multisport, nonstop endurance race and they surfaced on day one with strange horses forced in tail-to-nose proximity by overamped riders. One of the wranglers joked in passing: "Five percent of these horses don't belong here. Ninety-five percent of the riders don't either." This was a harsh assessment of the talent in the saddle, considering that most teams began the ride-and-run with their best riders on horseback and their best runners on foot.

Racers left the horses behind after twenty-six miles and plunged into icy water in the Upper and Lower Black Box Canyons for eighteen miles of swimming and wading. From the base of the canyon, the giant walls seemed to reach heaven. They also blocked the sun; hypothermia took several people out of the race.

The worst part followed: navigating over 109 miles of desert. It would have been hard if the maps were accurate, but it became impossible for most teams when they found that the two streams on the map, their intended water sources, had dried up.

The heat and lack of water hit Team Gold's Gym hard. They were among the handful of teams that had pushed aggressively early in the race and were in third place coming into the desert trek. Eric Henrion, a three-time veteran of the Raid Gauloise, had to stop. His teammate, Cathy Sassin, remembers looking at Eric getting more and more dehydrated.

Eric got heat exhaustion. He passed out and was down on the ground, unable to move. Dry heaves. There was nothing in him to throw up. We put a space blanket on him in the middle of the scorching desert. Nowhere to hide, and he's shivering with dry heaves, then unconscious for a while. We had choices. First of all, you can set your beacon off and get help. The team could certainly have had an attitude about it: "Oh, my God, we're out of the race." But that didn't happen. He told us what to do. He felt as long as he did not continue to get worse, that he was not going to quit. So we stayed in there and constantly assessed his status. We sat in the same spot for six hours. We were in third place at the time. Not one team passed us. So six hours later, the team had such a good attitude about it. We thought, if Eric is feeling this way right now, everyone else in this race is feeling this way right now.

Cathy had raced before, but this was her first experience with a situation like this. She held her teammate, massaged his legs, and tried to make him more comfortable. Eventually, he said, "Let's go."

We picked up his pack and walked alongside him, three inches at a time. We continued to walk and he felt as long as he could put one foot in front of the other, there was no reason to stop.

So we kept moving with him, that slowly, until I personally realized that I could die. My tongue was swollen. I couldn't swallow. Nobody could talk. I was so dehydrated I realized that this is how people die of dehydration. We got to the second spot on the map where there was supposed to be water. When we reached the first spot and there was no water, it was such a discouraging feeling. We had so much hope that we would get some little bit of water and it was dry, but we had a tiny glimmer of hope for the next stream. We got to that one and it was dry. The team felt crushed. We thought, no way, we can't survive this.

We looked up and there was a well on the top of a hill, so we thought, it's our only option. So we went up to check the well and it was dry. Next to the well was a mud pit with cattle hoofprints all over it, and this little, teeny film of muddy water, with a film on top that looked like an oil slick and a dead rat in the corner. It totally amazed me how the human body works. That, to us, was water.

They filtered the puddle through a scarf and added iodine. They had to drink it, knowing it would make them sick. Their bodies were forcing them to survive. They drank the water, sips at a time, and predictably, got diarrhea. But they continued to move forward slowly, with no one passing them.

In the meantime, some of the teams behind them that had managed to stay in the race found a well polluted with rat feces. They made the same choice as Team Gold's Gym and many got the same result. (Organizers had a hard time enforcing their promise to the Bureau of Land Management that racers would carry out their waste.)

Finally, Team Gold's Gym made it to a water source and sat for four hours, taking little sips until they were rehydrated enough to feel normal. Eric's troubles weren't over, though. After a short bike leg, they tackled the largest ropes course in the world—starting with a 440-foot overhanging rappel—then hiked to the river and set out on the white-water phase of the race.

People went over either the first or second set of rapids without scouting them and boats were everywhere. There was mayhem.

RACERS IN THE UTAH ECO-CHALLENGE BEGAN THE LONGEST ROPE
COURSE EVER CREATED WITH A 440-FOOT FREE RAPPEL.

People, paddles, everyone swept up by the water and onto the rocks. Our boat didn't flip, but we were negotiating the rapids and there was a guy from the Hewlett-Packard team [the eventual winners] who looked like he was drowning. So we tried to pull him into the boat at the same time we were trying to get through the rapids. As we hit a rock, Eric was thrown into the front of the boat. His shoulder hit the wrong way and he dislocated his shoulder. He was lying in the boat with his arm twisted in a disgustingly awkward position, screaming in pain. There's nothing we could do for him because if you stop paddling, everyone's out of the boat, and he's going to be swimming with one arm. So he lay there in pain and we eddied out as soon as we could. He rolled over, popped his own shoulder back in place, and lay on the bottom of the boat for the rest of the whitewater trip.

After the white water, a calm paddle took them to the base of a 1,200-foot cliff rising out of the Colorado River. Ropes had been set on the jagged face; they allowed racers to use ascending devices to climb up the dozen pitches and traverse around overhanging sections. Eric did it all, with his pack, with one arm.

If he had wanted to quit, we totally understood why, but if he continued to move forward, it was our job to make his life easier.

From then on in that race, and from every other race I was ever in after that, I realized what a person can actually go through. I think not many people push themselves through it to find out what's on the other side. The other side is, the sun comes up and it's a new day and you don't feel that way anymore.

Team Gold's Gym took third place in that race, just three hours and twenty minutes behind the winners and nearly two full days in front of the last team to cross the finish line.

Fuel for Going Up, Down, and Long

Nutrition is science, but your only test in the subject is whether or not you have enough energy for your activity. Start with the premise that everyone has the same fundamental nutritional needs. Add to that premise the fact that some needs change depending on the intensity and duration of an activity.

THE Republic of Mali is a large, landlocked chunk of West Africa located in the Sahel, the transitional zone between the Sahara to the north and tropical Africa to the south. It is the fourth poorest country on that continent. Food is often scarce and relentless seasonal winds whip every living thing with sand, debris, and fecal matter. Virtually no one except Todd Skinner and his free-climbing friends would see the remotest parts of Mali as a playground, and they were lured by only one thing: a rock formation called the Hand of Fatima. Unfortunately, the alluring towers were nowhere near a steady food supply.

We made a classic error by looking at a map of Mali and seeing the name Hombori in big letters.

The letters on the map were almost the same size as those used for the capital city, and we assumed we could get food there. We didn't buy much food going in because Hombori was only sixteen kilometers away from the site.

Hombori was just mud. On Tuesdays, there was a market that sold 90 percent everything but food. And we never knew what kind of food we could get, so we had to forage through the villages in the area and buy anything they would sell. That took a lot of time because the villages aren't very close to each other and they were really little, about twenty mud huts in each village.

Walking into some of the villages after dark created a scene. They of course had no electricity and maybe one oil-burning lamp in the whole village. We would come in with headlamps and scare the hell out of these people. We'd finally get their trust enough for one of the people to come out and we'd see their heads sticking out. We'd talk about food and try to relax a little bit. Sometimes we'd get food, sometimes we wouldn't. Sometimes they just didn't have it. We came between millet crops, so it was a lean time for everybody.

We'd buy chickens, eggs, goats. We came through one village and bought a bunch of eggs, then we came through later and bought a bunch of chickens. Then, almost at the end, we were dying because we couldn't get any more, so we went back to that village and tried to buy eggs again. They gently made us understand that wasn't possible—we'd already bought all their chickens.

> **If you think you'll need eggs,
> don't kill the chickens.**

Todd is usually in charge of food for his whole group and he places a lot of emphasis on things that had a mother—hence his dogged pursuit of chickens and goats in Mali. From his experience and that of his teams, he's found that climbers on big walls for weeks at a time—sometimes at high altitudes—perform better by making protein the central element of their diet. Jared Ogden, whose ascents of Shipton Spire and Great Sail Peak on Baffin Island launched him to the top ranks of big-wall pioneers, emphasizes protein as well to aid recovery.

Contrast Carolyn "Curly" Curl's nutritional trick just before she spends seconds speed skiing down the course in Vars, France: she downs an energy drink that pumps caffeine and B vitamins into her system. Tom Mason, who made the *Guinness Book* for his street luge speed record, takes the same approach. Killing a goat wouldn't help them go any faster.

During a week or more of nonstop adventure racing, Cathy Sassin never knows precisely what the physical requirements around the corner are. She has to have consistent energy levels plus the ability to expend power in short bursts. Cathy relies on her body's stored fat throughout the race, and her ability to do that is linked to her prerace eating habits. What she eats during a competition helps in specific ways, but isn't nearly as critical as what and how she ate in the months before the race began.

And then there are the eating challenges linked to high-altitude mountaineering and high-altitude rock and ice climbing. What do you eat when you have no appetite because of the altitude and, regardless of what you eat, your body will start to deteriorate because of the lack of oxygen? Not only that, but most everything freezes or hardens to a rocklike state.

Three categories of questions arise from these scenarios:

1. What are the general guidelines for high-performance eating?
2. What considerations related to the activity change the mix of nutrients required to achieve high performance?
3. What supplements work and when do they help most?

> The basic metabolic equation is
> food + oxygen = CO_2 + water + ATP (energy).
> ATP (adenosine triphosphate) is
> the body's fuel. Muscles will not
> work without it.

Guidance for All Athletes

Scott Connelly, MD, whose metabolic research helped save patients wasting away from illness before it focused on elite athletes, looks at human evolution for clues to what people should eat. He believes there's a basic mismatch between what people are designed to consume and what the modern food supply provides. One of these mismatches is the overabundance of and overemphasis on breads and cereals—the wide bottom of the food pyramid produced by the U.S. Department of Agriculture. Another is the inclusion of so many dairy products. Dr. Connelly asserts that modern humans evolved to a reasonable facsimile of what they are today prior to the development of agriculture and animal husbandry 10,000 years ago.

There is no magical disconnect between evolution and metabolism. Our brain size and complexity reflects billions of years of evolution, but the liver is the same liver as 10,000 years ago when agriculture came into being. It's impossible to suggest that any significant genetic change has occurred at the level of metabolism to account and deal with the perversion of the natural food supply that has occurred, first and foremost with agriculture. On top of that, 200 years ago industrialization brought processing into the picture. All of this has added up to task the system beyond its limits for metabolic transformation.

From the standpoint of what your system understands, the food pyramid is nonsense. Among the six food groups, two didn't exist throughout most of human history. Dairy and bread/cereals are not required.

In short, humans managed to form large brains and discover new lands, without cheese and crackers. Humans have relied on foods from the other four groups in the pyramid, however: animal and nonanimal sources of protein, vegetables, fruits, and fats. In *Mastering the Zone,* which includes sample meals for high-performance athletes, Barry Sears redesigns the food pyramid. In his version, water is the large foundation instead of bread and grains, fruits and vegetables form the next layer up, above that is low-fat protein, next is monounsaturated fats (e.g., olive oil), and finally, the triangle at the top is composed of breads, grains, starches, and pasta.*

To complicate the nutritional challenge, like most other large mammals, humans metabolize on a continuous basis. There is no switch that turns the metabolic engines on when people eat, or turns them off afterward to wait for the next fuel delivery. This fact presents a challenge for anyone. People need to eat in a manner that provides the necessary raw materials for these biochemical processes, or the organs and functions that need those materials will take them from other places in the body. The tissue that's affected most by this is muscle. The brain, for example, survives on glucose, and if it doesn't get enough it will "steal" it from muscle. It will break down muscle so it can continue to function.

Another part of the equation relates to quantity as well as quality of fuel. As athletes build muscle, their caloric requirements increase. In essence, the more muscle they have the more calories they need per

*Barry Sears, *Mastering the Zone* (HarperCollins, 1997), p. 51.

day. And ideally, those calories will come from nutrient-dense foods—foods with lots of nutrients per kilocalorie.

Athletes also need to consider the role of supplements in their diet as well as performance-enhancing foods developed to send a certain "metabolic message." To shortcut to the bottom line, if athletes don't eat things well suited for high performance, then they won't achieve their highest performance.

Cathy Sassin had frustrating results by following conventions regarding the amount of carbohydrates, proteins, and fats in her diet. With a degree in exercise physiology and a mother and sister who are registered dietitians, she thought she knew what to eat for high performance. For years, she followed the typical diet that she had as a college athlete: high in complex carbohydrates, low in protein, low to no fat. During her college years, she had 25 percent body fat while working out four times a day.

> I had major energy fluctuations throughout the day. I would get really tired and had to eat. I would constantly crave pasta, rice, and bread, bread, bread. Performance-wise I was fine. It wasn't until I went into personal training that I realized how much nutrition played a role in a person's overall performance.
>
> I started manipulating my own ratios of proteins, fats, carbs, and calories. I did that for a while and went from 25 to 19 percent body fat and my performance increased, but I still had mood swings and energy fluctuations throughout the day. I would get weak and tired and constantly have cravings for things.

Cathy revamped her diet again after going back to basic physiologic principles such as those mentioned above. She started eating roughly every three hours throughout the day, relying more on lean protein and always including a very small amount of "good" fat—a little olive oil, for example—to her meal.

If you don't balance things properly and you eat a high complex carbohydrate diet, your body is becoming more efficient at storing fat than it is at using it. That's counterproductive. We want the body to mobilize that fat out of storage, get it into the bloodstream where it can be accessed and gotten into the muscle and converted to energy. Then your performance goes up.

The goal is to balance proteins and carbohydrates so you have the carbohydrates you need to produce the fuel (for example, ATP) for metabolic functions, and you have the protein you need to be able to stimulate the enzymes to mobilize the fat from storage. It takes some experimentation, rather than a rigid formula, for each individual to get the ratios of proteins, carbohydrates, and fats right so the body consistently has a normal blood sugar level and the brain is stimulated to understand that it's constantly getting what it needs. Eating small amounts four to six times a day also requires some rethinking and preparation.

Todd and his team usually consume 5,000 to 6,000 calories a day during a climb. He calls it "shoveling coal. You just try to delay the damage and promote the energy so you can finish the task at hand." Even so, when Todd is on the wall for days or weeks at a time, or when Cathy is racing for ten days nonstop, it is almost impossible for them to consume calories equal to the amount of energy they are expending. If they couldn't access their fat stores efficiently, their brains would force the degeneration of their muscle mass at a rapid rate; their health, as well as their success, is at stake.

> You can eat junk, but if you're eating
> high-value foods at the same time,
> you will be a better athlete than
> if you eat nothing but junk.

Four Basics on Eating for High Performance

1. Drink water throughout the day and eat a lot of water-rich carbohydrates like fresh fruits and vegetables.
2. Have a lean source of protein with every meal—trim fat off your meat, toss out the egg yolks and eat the whites, remove skin from chicken and fish.
3. At each meal, add a small amount of fat that is mostly monounsaturated, like a tablespoon of olive or canola oil, a few almonds, or some avocado slices. (Note: the major sources of "bad" fats— saturated fats—in most diets are meats and whole milk dairy products.)
4. Have small meals throughout the day—four, five, or even six. You'll feel better than eating huge meals a couple of times a day.

Guidance According to Activity

As the examples above indicate, extreme sports make demands on the system in myriad ways. The energy requirements for performance include:

♦♦♦ Short bursts (ninety seconds or less) of high intensity. Freeflyers, skateboarders, and other athletes doing "tricks" have this requirement for quick action and fast response. So do athletes in many speed sports, like boardercross and street luge.

In short-duration activities, ATP goes very quickly. And because the muscles are working so hard so fast, they rely primarily on anaerobic ("without oxygen") systems to get a sufficient supply of ATP, whereas athletes in lower-intensity, longer-duration activities rely mostly on the aerobic ("with oxygen") system. Energy production needs are met by the aerobic system only when adequate oxygen is delivered into the cells.

This bit of science is important because it determines the food and supplements that most effectively replenish the energy supply.

◆◆◆　High intensity for ninety seconds to an hour. Certain mountain biking races, competitive ice climbing, or ocean kayaking in a rock garden would fit in this category.

These athletes use a combination of energy systems. The ATP is used very quickly, so there is reliance on the anaerobic pathway, but they get some aerobic energy production in there as well. It's important for them to make sure that, in order to have sufficient energy at performance time, their gut is empty of foods that require a lot of digestive enzymes. For example, the night before a race is a bad time to have a huge steak because it will sit in the digestive system. They need to eat foods that will transition out, but deliver a lot of energy, such as lots of fresh vegetables and a serving of lean chicken or fish that's no bigger than the palm of the hand.

◆◆◆　Endurance activities requiring short, intense bursts. A long ice climb or free climb would involve periodic power moves. An adventure race would mix it up like this for more than week.

Cathy Sassin described the challenge perfectly: "programming" the body before the activity is paramount. It is essential in an activity like this to be able to draw on the body's own fat stores, then use the available food supply to provide the extra energy boost required for the short-term, intense activity.

◆◆◆　Endurance at relatively low altitudes. Racing across the Sahara falls in this category.

ADVENTURE RACERS COMMONLY USE A TYROLEAN TRAVERSE FOR RIVER AND CANYON CROSSINGS. IN CONTRAST TO THE HOURS OF STEADY EFFORT DURING AN ADVENTURE RACE, THIS MOVE REQUIRES A BURST OF ENERGY.

Again, the ability to draw on the body's stores is critical. It must also be combined with a pattern of hydration that fits the activity.

◆◆◆ Endurance at high altitudes. Climbing mountains like Everest, K2, Kanchenjunga, and even the nontechnical Kilimanjaro has distinct challenges.

Any individual adapted to sea level who climbs to heights over 18,000 feet will see a rapid wasting of their muscles regardless of how much they eat. The diminished oxygen supply causes the body to continuously deplete the glucose that's stored in the muscles and the liver, or glycogen. As the body continues to try to maintain the ATP generation required for life, the process of glycogen repletion keeps taking certain amino acids that are needed for the process out of the muscles. At that point, according to Scott Connelly, "It doesn't matter how much energy you feed the person, as long as those amino acids are lacking, they'll continue to be cannibalized from existing muscle tissue stores and this is the reason why those people waste."

Traditionally, alpine climbers travel with calorie-dense foods like animal fat, but that does not stop the wasting process, as so many have discovered. By trial and error, some of these athletes have discovered things that seem to help, however, and they are products that go right to the heart of the amino acid challenge. They include items like sweetened condensed milk and certain types of so-called engineered foods, both of which are discussed later.

Supplements

Some supplements are either bogus or the amount of useful ingredient is so pitifully small in the product that it has negligible value. In some cases, the reason certain supplements have secured a reputation among athletes is more related to legend than research. It's the placebo effect at work. Ginseng enjoyed a surge in popularity in the 1970s when Russian scientists alleged that it was one of the secrets to their Olympic athletes' stamina, strength, and concentration, but research on its merits is still going on.

On the other hand, some supplements clearly make a difference in performance and have proven that fact in studies that included control groups taking placebos. Among extreme athletes, these are some of the most popular and efficacious:

◆◆◆ *Caffeine.* It is impossible to ignore the performance-enhancing benefits of this stimulant for short-term, intense activities: the most popular beverages at extreme sports competitions all contain caffeine (that's not necessarily an endorsement). Based on research, an acceptable dosage relationship of caffeine to body weight is about 3 mg/kg. A cup of coffee contains roughly 120 mg of caffeine, so a 170-pound athlete should be able to have a couple of cups without jitteriness, heart palpitations, dizziness, or anxiety. Always know exactly how much you're consuming and avoid the temptation to combine it with any other stimulant like ephedra, or expect the negative side effects. Also be aware that caffeine does more harm than good for people with certain types of diseases. Athletes with circulation problems, for example, should avoid it because it is a vasoconstrictor. It can also dry out athletes— hydration is critical to performance—and throw off the energy balance.

◆◆◆ *Chondroitin.* Joint pain and cartilage damage plague athletes of all ages, so it's a good idea to consider taking naturally occurring substances like chondroitin sulfates and glucosamine to mitigate the problems. Chondroitin aids joint lubrication and there is speculation that it actually restores lost cartilage. *Earl Mindell's Supplement Bible,* a straightforward guide to hundreds of natural products, says the right amount is two 500 mg tablets or capsules twice daily.*

◆◆◆ *Creatine.* Earlier in this chapter there were references to the aerobic and the anaerobic chemical reactions that replenish ATP. One of the sources of anaerobic ATP production is creatine phosphate, an amino acid. The body can break it down quickly to help generate ATP, but muscles don't store it well. Athletes who need short bursts of energy will most likely benefit from supplementing their diet with creatine in the weeks prior to an event, but they should be sure to drink more water throughout the time they take it. The normal recommended dosage of creatine is 5 grams/day.

◆◆◆ *HMB (Beta-hydroxy Beta-methylbutyrate).* This is another substance that the body itself contains. It's a by-product of the body's normal breakdown of leucine, an amino acid. As in the case of creatine, the theory is that supplementing the body's own supply will enhance performance; in this case, it will help build muscle and decrease body fat. Scott Connelly asserts that HMB improves maximal oxygen carrying capacity (VO_2 max) and will also provide "a short-chain fatty acid substrate for suppression of glucose oxidation during the long haul so that you spare glucose and use more fat." It's intended to be used with vigorous exercise, though, and in the absence of it, you may see no results from using it.

With years of research to back up his assertions, Dr. Connelly warns athletes about being duped by endorsements and product claims:

It's important to be very precise and establish criteria of adequacy to assess the impact of any one single supplement. If I give HMB to somebody, I can tell you precisely what's going to happen and what

*Earl Mindell *Earl Mindell's Supplement Bible* (Simon & Schuster, 1998).

the end benefit will be. If I give creatine to somebody, I can tell you what threshold level of saturation you have to achieve to get the benefit. I can tell you how to get that, I can tell you what the average benefit will be, and I have a molecular explanation for it that is highly plausible. You can't do that with most of these hocus-pocus things that people latch on to.

Kevin Maselka, a conditioning specialist who has trained many superstar athletes, also encourages every athlete to look beyond the claims and find out what studies were done on the product and where they were published. A study published in *The New England Journal of Medicine,* for example, has been peer-reviewed and has credibility, but some company-sponsored "studies" are published in so-called journals that print almost anything. Those pages of misleading and bogus research include many Web pages, so beware. Appendix A lists some Web sites that may be helpful in finding reliable information.

In reviewing the energy requirements of different kinds of extreme athletes, Kevin offers the following tips on eating and supplementation. These guidelines highlight what many of the athletes have discovered through personal experience, and they apply in a practical way what metabolic researchers like Scott Connelly say about the various food groups and supplements.

First, two general cautions:

1. Don't radically alter your diet or introduce supplements just before a competition or major activity, thinking that will rectify bad habits. You could get sick, or weaken yourself to the point where you lose energy and your performance drops. The key is to combine these recommended components in a nutritional program so that, over time, they are balanced, the body is acclimated to this new eating pattern, and you can predictably boost your energy when you need to do that.

2. If you have had health problems in the past that give you the slightest reason to believe that introducing a new supplement to your system or changing your diet could harm you, see a doctor first, not a lawyer later.

All Athletes

♦♦♦ Proper *hydration* is the foundation of any high-performance nutritional program. Drink half your body weight in ounces of water. So, if you weight 150 pounds, you need 75 ounces or about nine big glasses of water. If you drink alcohol or caffeine products or if you take creatine, increase the amount of water to keep your energy high. If you have a lot of fresh fruits and vegetables in your diet, they help hydrate you so you may need less water. Two major signs point to lack of sufficient hydration: fatigue and yellow urine. Constipation is a big hint, too.

♦♦♦ Under most circumstances, *protein* is more important for recovery of your muscles than it is as an energy source. Ingesting sufficient protein also makes you less susceptible to injuries in various tissues—muscles, tendons, ligaments.

♦♦♦ Go *back to nature for your carbohydrates* as much as possible. Eat fresh fruits and vegetables and stay away from white flour and processed foods. And when it comes to so-called complex carbohydrates, generally speaking, put a little color in your diet: eat brown rice instead of white; sweet potatoes instead of white potatoes. The former have more fiber and a lower glycemic index than the white ones. That means they will deliver a steadier stream of energy, rather than cause an energy spike.

♦♦♦ Take a *multivitamin* or put together a multivitamin pack that suits your needs. It's insurance. Avoid the hard tablet vitamins, unless you like to chew them; the body absorbs the chelated kind more easily. Capsules are even better. A specific need for antioxidants (vitamins A, C, and E, selenium, and lipoic acid) arises as one of the effects of exercise. Working out burns oxygen; that produces free radicals, which contribute to the stiff or sore feeling that follows a brutal training session or contest. Antioxidants should help your recovery.

✦✦✦ Add *chondroitin sulfate and/or glucosamine* to your diet to help protect your joints.

Nutrition Tips for
Different Kinds of Athletes

Athletes in Short-Duration Sports (Ninety Seconds or Less)

✦✦✦ Rely primarily on *lean sources of protein,* rather than fatty meats that bog down the digestive process.

✦✦✦ Two weeks prior to an event or a hard training cycle, try *creatine loading.* Add up to 20 grams a day to your diet until the event is over, then stop until you approach another competition. Take note: this loading dose is four times higher than the normal recommended daily amount and the correct dose is somewhat weight-dependent, so it's good to experiment during a training cycle rather than begin just before a contest.

✦✦✦ It is vital to include a balance of fresh fruits and vegetables to ensure adequate supply of *micronutrients and enzymes* to break down the carbohydrates into the proper fuel level that you're going to be utilizing in your sport. These enzymes and nutrients will enable you to replenish ATP quickly. And, yes, fruits and vegetables help hydrate you and give you essential fiber. Kevin cautions:

Fibrous foods are key. You don't want food sitting in your intestines during a competition. If you have a guy who's eating nothing but cheeseburgers or heavy fat foods, he'll have a gut full of red meat because he has very little fiber in his diet. High fat, red meat slows an athlete down, can accumulate, and will produce more of those vacillations in energy that you want to avoid. You want to establish a consistent nutritional program, so you can replicate that during competition without interference.

You can win and eat burgers and pizza every day, but why not take it one level higher and perform even better?

Athletes in High-Intensity Endurance Sports (Ninety Seconds to an Hour)

◆◆◆ Like athletes in short-burst activities, choose *lean sources of protein* rather than a lot of red meat, which is harder to digest. Cow's milk and other dairy products are also hard to digest and they interfere with digestion of other nutrients that are more important for a race. Pistol Pete Loncarevich is one top competitor who avoids dairy products and sugar. Kevin notes that:

On average, 10 percent of the calories you eat go to digestion. If you take in 1,000 calories, and 10 percent of them are used for digestion, you only have the balance left for the race before you start to deplete your stores, and it becomes a less-efficient means of fueling you. Eat efficient types of food.

◆◆◆ Pay attention to the above recommendations on *fruits and vegetables.*

◆◆◆ *Creatine* can also be useful for athletes in this category.

Athletes in Endurance Activities Requiring Occasional Quick Bursts

◆◆◆ Review Cathy Sassin's eating program, described above, which is geared toward making the body a fat-burning, rather than a fat-storing, machine. Her frequent meals feature lean protein sources and high-fiber sources of carbohydrates, but also include small amounts of fat such as a tablespoon of peanut butter or olive oil.

◆◆◆ Avoid the temptation to introduce caffeine or other stimulants at the time during the event when explosive energy is needed; it could throw off the energy balance you need after that.

◆◆◆ During the event, carry *light, nutrient-dense foods.* Cathy Sassin's staples for adventure races include ostrich and turkey jerky, both low-fat protein sources; roll-ups and bars made solely from fruit; trail mix; nuts; almond paste; and prepackaged dehydrated foods.

◆◆◆ During the event, also give yourself some *treats.* The best adventure racers agree with this wholeheartedly: the psychological boost you get from a "fun food" can outweigh the nutritional merits of one more energy bar or carb cocktail. When Team Eco-Internet competed in—and later won—the Eco-Challenge in British Columbia, their support crew had Domino's drive sixty miles to deliver fresh pizzas to the team when they arrived at a transition area.

Ultraracers and Other Endurance Athletes Performing at Relatively Low Altitudes

◆◆◆ Before the activity get in the habit of *hydrating in the same pattern* that you will use during the event or competition. If you will be drinking several ounces of water every twenty minutes, then follow that pattern in the weeks prior to the race so your body knows exactly what to expect.

◆◆◆ Focus on *carbohydrate intake,* not to the exclusion of protein, but certainly carbs play a more major role in sustaining energy in something like a race across the Sahara.

High-Altitude Climbers These recommendations come exclusively from the athletes themselves because they have firsthand knowledge of what works or, at the very least, what works well enough to keep them alive. Metabolic theories support some of their hard-won discoveries.

Heidi Howkins, who led an international 1998 K2 expedition and 1999 Everest expedition, enriches her diet prior to climbs over 25,000 feet with iron and vitamin C: "Three to five months prior, make sure available iron is as high as possible. You will deplete your hemoglobin on the mountain, so you have to build up in advance." She also recommends having hemoglobin levels measured during that period to maintain the desired level.

At high altitudes, climbers have no access to fresh fruits and vegetables and, even at base camp, protein can be hard to get. There is no refrigeration and it gets warm on the glacier during the day. Temperatures fluctuate wildly. Normally, the climbers wouldn't see directly how this affects their base camp food supply, but on Heidi's 1998 K2 expedition, the cook was helicoptered off the mountain with a kidney stone, so the climbers had to cook for themselves for a few days.

> We developed a profound appreciation for the number of ways that eggs can go bad—gray ones, fluorescent green ones. We discovered the cook wasn't as careful as we were about picking the good ones. Here's a risk on the mountain we hadn't expected: salmonella.

That particular risk disappears when the climbers leave base camp because they usually leave their protein behind. At the higher altitudes, their appetite decreases; the only things Heidi is able to ingest are simple carbohydrates.

> The only thing I carry on a summit bid is drink powder and PowerGel. Only things that don't freeze above 26,000 feet. I've also tried sweetened condensed milk. At really extreme altitudes, you

can't eat anything that will draw moisture from your stomach because it will make you feel queasy.

Not all climbers agree, however. On the mountain, certain cultural traditions supersede science or other climbers' wisdom.

Ukrainian climbers had what was essentially fat slathered in mustard. A block of homemade horsefat—a solid cube of fat that had a baconsized sliver of meat in it. They had melted it at home in Odessa and served it with mustard that came in a vitamin bottle.

And the French, she says, prefer their blocks of fat in the form of cheese—a treat that French teams have also been known to carry on adventure races.

Scott Connelly believes that Heidi's approach makes more sense.

Sweetened condensed milk might be helpful at high altitude because its amino acid spectrum is more appropriate than that of a chicken breast, for example, but fat is an oxidative fuel and the problem at altitude is that a greater proportion of your metabolism is driven without oxygen.

Todd Skinner's historic free climb of Trango Tower's (also called Nameless Tower) East Face brought his team up to 20,469 feet. The altitude and elements brutalized them during their two months on the wall: "We came in with a huge level of power, knowing that it would be taken away from us day by day."

We used engineered food, especially MET-Rx, because it stopped the catabolism [breakdown] from happening and kicked up recovery. It saved us on Trango. You don't have to cook it and it's high-quality calories. Any time we had a chance, we would melt the snow and make a pudding. We threw M&Ms in to make it attractive, just so we could keep good food coming in.

The final lesson on eating for success is making sure that your post-contest or post-event diet supports total recovery. For this, protein is critical in repairing microtears in muscles, tendons, and ligaments.

PARAGLIDING INTO GUINNESS

Objective: Stay in the air and ride thermals like hawks. But don't just circle in a field. Catch a thermal, then go to the top of it, glide, and find another one before hitting the ground. That's cross-country flying. Sometimes, it's easy to catch one of those rising columns of air and take it up to 18,000 feet, or 20,000 feet, or even higher. Hawks don't carry portable oxygen; paragliders do.

A fully equipped paraglider pilot looks like a space man. It's hard for people hanging out in shorts and T-shirts to understand why Will Gadd is near them dressed in a one-piece down suit, balaclava, and goggles, with an oxygen hose on his nose.

Will was fully prepared for the freezing temperatures more than three miles above the ground when he left Hobbs, a town in western New Mexico, and headed cross country toward Amarillo, Texas, to try to set a world paragliding record. If he got that far, it would be a 180-mile flight and he would break the world record of 174.9 miles, which had stood for six years.

At 18,000 feet it can be well below freezing. You've got your mitts on, GPS (Global Positioning System), flight computer, variometer—it's like an altimeter, telling you to the foot how high you are and what rate you're ascending or descending. The GPS ties into a flight computer, which tells you your glide angle. There's lots of technology involved in the sport. You can easily be standing on the hill with $10,000 worth of toys.

Paragliding began in France as a relatively inexpensive and highly risky stunt. People just took some of the early square parachuting canopies of the late 1970s and early 1980s and flew them off steep hillsides. With the canopy redesigned specifically for flight rather than descent, and with the addition of gadgets, the sport of paragliding was born. The modifications didn't mean that the risk was removed, however. It just meant that paragliders could explore greater heights and longer flights and assume new types of risk.

A paragliding wing can glide at a ratio of ten to one—for every foot it drops, it goes forward ten feet—and it has a descent rate of less than three feet a second. This means it gets twenty times the lateral travel of a modern skydiving canopy, which drops two feet for every one foot it goes forward. Also, the descent rate of a parachute is about twenty-one feet a second. In short, a paragliding wing is now much more a device made to fly than it is a descent tool. Some of the pilots aim for long cross-country flights like Will. Others soar from one ridge to another, primarily along the West Coast of the United States. Some pilots focus on paragliding competitions, in which they launch off a mountain and follow a course with predetermined checkpoints. In flying over the point, which might be a peak or lake, the competitor photographs it. Whoever makes it around the course first, or the most times, wins.

Will's starting place for his world record attempt was an old airport largely abandoned except for hang gliders, sail planes, and paragliders who have disregarded warnings that wind conditions at Hobbs are too strong for them. Will determined that he and his equipment could handle those conditions easily.

During the record attempts, he and a friend had a daily routine: fly as far as possible, pack the wing in a truck, drive back to the airport, then do it again. In some ways, launching the paraglider is like flying a kite. The truck tows the wing down the runway and, as it climbs higher, the vehicle lets out more line. Often the paraglider gets towed to 500 or even 1,000 feet before finding a good thermal and releasing the line.

On May 30, 1998, one of those tows led to a six-and-a-half-hour flight to Texas. The whole time Will was airborne, he continually had to make tactical decisions.

If I fly over there, will that cloud give me lift? Will that brown field over there work better, or maybe that red field? Where are the thermals going to be? It's like playing chess in the air. You have to make all these tactical decisions about what is going to work best on that day. My main memories of that flight are getting fairly low—maybe a few hundred feet off the ground—and finding a massive dusty devil that's ripping all this red dirt into the air.

Dust devils are whirlwinds that form when extreme surface-heating conditions cause a layer of unstable air to form close to the ground. Usually, they don't last more than fifteen minutes, but the vortex is powerful, rotating at speeds up to fifty miles an hour. A dust devil has killed at least one skydiver and it could do the same to a paraglider. In this case, Will rode it up: "This was a big one and it was quite strong, so I went from maybe a couple hundred feet over the ground to about 12,000 feet above the ground in about ten minutes." In other words, he got to that altitude about as fast as if he'd been riding in a turbine aircraft. Right after this, Will hit a three-hour stretch of good luck.

About noon that day, all these cumulus clouds started popping. That's like powder for a skier. A paraglider sees that and knows conditions are getting good. All of a sudden the whole sky popped like popcorn and I started getting really good thermals, from that point to about three o'clock. I didn't have to work very hard. I was just going from cloud to cloud at about 10,000 feet above the ground. I remember that so well.

After that, he had to start working hard for his record. There were big forest fires in Mexico and the smoke from them was filling the atmosphere above his flight path on the high-altitude winds, perhaps 40,000 or 50,000 feet above ground level. The smoke obscured the sun and significantly reduced thermal activity.

That smoke caught up to me and I spent the rest of the flight very, very low to the ground. At one point, I was down to telephone wire height. I was on the upwind edge of this field and fairly strong winds were blowing—thirty miles an hour on the ground. With the canopy in a safe configuration, you can make it go faster than thirty, but it's very unstable. You don't want to do that low to the ground. You don't want to lose your canopy low to the ground.

At thirty miles an hour—my wing cruises at twenty-five miles per hour—I was going backward. I was at the upwind edge of the field, going backward, and a small dust devil, maybe the size of a small room, came through. There were farmworkers in the field. They were yelling at me in Spanish something about landing. I thought I *was* going to land.

I finally caught this small dust devil and that got me back up to a couple thousand feet above the ground. That happened repeatedly. It was hot down there, and I'm dressed in this high-altitude down suit. So it was about 100 degrees on the ground and I'm dressed for 15,000 feet. I spent about two hours battling like this. It was completely physically exhausting keeping my wing turned up on edge in these itty-bitty thermals, but that worked. That's what made the record possible that day.

I was especially happy, because if it had been a perfect day and I just floated along the cloud base for hours and gotten the record, I would have been happy, but I was really happy to get it under what were more difficult conditions.

A year later on June 8, 1999, Will also set the U.S. tandem record in a flight with his friend Kim Czismazia, a world-class athlete also featured in this book.

> If you're falling out of the sky,
> the thing to do is figure out how
> to stop falling and not worry about
> the sudden stop at the bottom.

WILL GADD CALLS HIS PARAGLIDING HARNESS "A FLYING LA-Z-BOY." IT HAS PROTECTIVE FOAM PADDING AND PLACES FOR HIS OXYGEN SUPPLY, GPS, FLIGHT COMPUTER, AND OTHER GEAR. PHOTO BY S. TYLER YOUNG.

Training Tools—From Barbells to Microchips

CHAPTER 4

Once you identify an activity you want to improve in, look at the many types of training that will support your development. For example, weight training can build functional strength and help prevent injury. In some cases, specialized facilities or training tools give athletes distinct benefits both in competition and in outdoor adventures.

"WE'RE behind the crowd, setting up for a diamond dirty loop. Weeds, Wolfy, Gucci, comin' right, a little pull . . ."

Inside the cockpit of his F/A-18, Lieutenant Commander Mark Dunleavy hears the number one pilot, "the boss," call the formation in cadence and he prepares to do a hook-straining maneuver. It's a specialty of the U.S. Navy's Blue Angels, but no one from the ground can see it. He must do this maneuver before the onset of additional Gs or the blood will leave his brain. While he's doing it, he still has to fly the formation. And, since Mark's the number four pilot, or "slot man," he has to pay attention to the wingmen. They can't tell all the movement that's going on behind them, so part of Mark's job is to keep their wingtips from touching. Another part of his job as a slot is to know when to flush the maneuver if it goes badly. In other words, with a handful of life-or-death actions to take in a few seconds, this hook maneuver better be second nature and strong enough to keep him conscious.

When pilots pull against the force of gravity, all the blood in their head and upper body wants to go down to their toes. Blood leaves the brain, they pass out, eventually they could die. They can counter that by wearing G suits, which would automatically squeeze blood from the lower body to the upper body in response to the G forces, but they can also counter it by consciously tightening those parts of the body with a hook-straining maneuver.

Navy pilots flying tactical aircraft like the F/A-18 normally wear G suits *and* do a form of the hook, but not the Blue Angels. The G suits stay on the ground because of how they fly. Mark:

> We fly with four heavy springs attached to the stick. The stick is how I turn the jet—left, right, up, down. Those springs provide about thirty pounds of isometric pressure away from me, so if I let go of the stick, the jet would want to nosedive. The reason we fly with springs attached is that it helps reduce pilot-induced oscillation. It helps to smooth out your correction. It's one of the tools that helps us fly as tight and close as we do in the Blues and have all that wing overlap, and do those precise maneuvers that folks attribute to the Blues.
>
> So, in order to counter those springs—holding the thirty-pound weight for forty-five minutes to an hour and fifteen minutes really wipes your arm out—we fly with the rudder pedal all the way forward and we rest our arm on our thigh. Our thigh helps support our arm for the duration of the flight.

The G suit has an air bladder that wraps around the pilot's thighs. If a Blue Angel pilot wore one, every time he (they're all "he" at the moment) would pull a G, the bladder would fill with air, and since his arm is resting on it, that would move his arm. That, in turn, would move the stick, making it impossible to get as tight in formations as the Blues do. The jets are so close and the margin of error is so small, that even that little arm movement would be excessive. So the Blues have no G suits.

The Value of Weight Training in Unrelated Activities

To carry off a hook maneuver of the intensity they need to keep blood pumping into their brains, these pilots have to be in great anaerobic shape. They tighten all the major muscles of the body—abdomen, lower extremities, calves, butt muscles—and the figure K bend in the upper body helps to close the diaphragm. It's like straining hard on the toilet, but putting their legs into it, too.

Weight training in the gym is not optional. It's a part of the Blue Angels' routine five or six days a week to ensure they have sufficient strength for controlled movements and for powerful contractions when they need it. That's one of several main reasons why extreme athletes head for the gym to achieve peak performance.

Weight Training:
Why It Supports Peak Performance

+++ Power needed for certain moves;

+++ Ability to handle stresses on the body;

+++ Dense muscle mass to protect bones and organs during impact;

+++ Weight management; and

+++ Psychological edge of feeling strong and disciplined.

CASEY MEARS BLASTS THROUGH A PRACTICE RUN BEFORE A RACE AT THE NAZARETH SPEEDWAY IN PENNSYLVANIA. WEIGHT TRAINING HELPS HIM HANDLE HUGE STRESSES ON THE BODY AND BUILDS MUSCLE THAT PROTECTS HIM IN A CRASH.

Like the Blues, athletes who race cars or top-fuel boats need regular weight workouts, as well as cardiorespiratory training, to stay in control despite the huge stresses on their body.

Casey Mears, one of a third generation of Mears racers, has known since childhood what racing demands of a driver:

> The physical and mental stresses of racing are incredible. There is stress on the neck and shoulders—all upper body because of the Gs going around the corners. There's no power steering because it takes away feeling, so there's a lot of stress on the wheel.
>
> The most important reason to be fit in race car driving is that if you're physically tired, you won't be sharp mentally, then your driving is shot. You have to be physically fit so you don't get distracted when you should be thinking about taking a proper line through a corner and getting by the cars in front of you.

Casey can't spend a nanosecond feeling depleted or distracted from the tasks at hand. At Fontana and Michigan, two of the super-speedways where he races in the Indy Light circuit, drivers reach 200 miles an hour. Their reactions must be correspondingly fast. If someone crashes and a part flies onto the track, someone spins, or an engine quits so there's a slow car on the track, his motor control and response time will determine what happens to him.

Racers also need a weight training regimen to build a protective layer of muscle. Like lugers, skiers, and many other types of athletes focused on speed, they run a high risk of slamming into something. As Michael Shannon, longtime luger and race organizer, points out, "Sliding on pavement's not bad—your leathers protect you—it's when you hit a stationary object that you have a problem." Weight training builds the dense muscle mass that protects the bones and organs during impact.

Much to his dismay, Casey was able to test that theory in a

high-speed, three-car crash during the 1997 Indy Light Championship race in Fontana, California.

> I hit the wall at about 170. I was passing two guys on the outside and they lost it and started heading for the wall. I was between them and the wall and they picked me up and smashed me into the wall. The impact took off both sides of the car. It really messed up the car but the only things I had wrong with me physically were a little bump on my right hand and a little bruise on my right knee. Usually, when you get out of something like that, something's broken or at least you're really sore the next day. I wasn't and I think I owe that to working out.

A video of the accident indicated that there had been no way for Casey to steer around the problem. Athletes in supercross, boarder-cross, and other races with competitors in close proximity face an identical risk—that someone else will lose control. They all have to enter the race physically prepared to take a hit.

The likelihood of crashing in any of the "trick sports" makes it smart for those athletes to lift weights, too. Bicycle stunt rider Dave Mirra credits part of his resilience to his diligent weight training. Anyone who tries a double tail whip, spinning the bike 720 degrees in the air underneath him, is bound to miss the landing sometimes. Mirra's precedent-setting triple gold in the 1998 Summer X Games followed by two more golds in the 1999 games is evidence that he can withstand the crashes in practice enough to be in top form for the contests.

All of this makes sense, but why would skydivers find it necessary to weight-train *or* do cardio work? Jumping out of an airplane is not exactly an endurance sport and people don't get hurled into each other—do they? The short answer to the second question is, yes, they do. And the answer to the first is best expressed through the philosophy and training regimen of the world champion four-way team,* Arizona Airspeed.

Team member Dan Broksky-Chenfeld says his team believes "champions must be fit" and that fitness has distinct psychological benefits, as well as physical ones:

> When you're in the heat of battle, you can stand strong and mighty and realize you've worked harder than anyone else and that you're in the ideal physical condition for your sport. In contrast, you'll create a negative effect without the high level of fitness.

The surprise is not how the members of Airspeed stay fit, that is, the makeup of their routine, as much as it is how their routine helps them win. Their six-day-a-week program consists of (in order):

◆◆◆ Endurance (Cardiorespiratory) Training

The team meets at 5:00 A.M. in the summer and 6:00 A.M. in the winter and starts with forty minutes of running, riding a bicycle or exercise bike, or doing the StairMaster.

The sport itself does not require a great deal of endurance. A four-way team's practice jump normally lasts fifty seconds or less. The training and competition days are endurance *days,* though. At the national and world meets, it takes about twelve hours to do the six required jumps. Being fit for an endurance sport like long-distance running or biking makes the skydivers fit mentally and physically for those days.

---

*Four-way competition requires four jumpers to join together in specific formations during their skydive. A videographer records the round; it is subsequently judged on the basis of how many consecutively complete formations were achieved in thirty-five seconds.

◆◆◆   Stretching

The team does a thirty-minute stretching session developed through working with personal trainers. It encompasses full-body stretching, but emphasizes flexibility in the hips and legs, shoulders and arms, and chest—the areas that are the critical flying surfaces in skydiving.

Stretching is as crucial for a skydiver as it is for a gymnast or dancer. Moving the flying machines that are their bodies means they rely on the flexibility and control they have. The more flying surfaces they have to work with, the quicker control they have.

After stretching, the team takes twenty minutes to get their minds ready for the day ahead. There is no formal meditation program; this is personal.

◆◆◆   Skydiving

They do what they do best twelve times a day, that is, they exit an aircraft at about 10,000 feet and practice different formations. As a point of comparison, most skydivers would feel as if they'd put in a full and exhausting day at the drop zone after half as many jumps.

◆◆◆   Weight Training

At the end of the day, the team lifts weights for an hour, but not exactly together. Everyone has a different routine, depending on the desired outcome, which relates specifically to body weight— losing, maintaining, or gaining.

When the four first came together, three of them wore weight vests to skydive. These are vests of pockets loaded with lead to help

produce the weight (actually the fall-rate) differences between skydivers so they can more easily fly at the same level. But wearing a vest
restricts movement and adds to the time needed to get ready for a skydive, so it wouldn't work for Airspeed. The team threw away the easy
"solution," and began working toward their ideal weights. For some,
lifting became the tool to gain. Others just needed to maintain their
mass. Adjustments in their cardiorespiratory and eating routines com-
plement their approach with the weights, and they stay on the program
year round. Athletes in many other sports use weight lifting primarily to
make seasonal changes in body weight. For example, before her speed
skiing season Carolyn Curl, the women's world record holder, builds her
petite five feet two inches into 135 solid pounds by hefting heavy
weights while she eats lean protein "constantly." Off-season, Curly is
usually ten pounds lighter.

General Tips on Using Weight Training to Improve Performance

◆◆◆ If your aim is muscular endurance, train with relatively light loads.
Use weights with which you can do at least fifteen repetitions.

◆◆◆ If you want to gain power and build dense muscle mass, you
must lift loads heavy enough to challenge you. But never sacri-
fice good form just to "go heavy."

◆◆◆ Rely mainly on closed-chain exercises to build functional
strength. These are exercises like squats and lunges that use
the muscles in a weight-bearing position. (For example, you're
standing on the floor while working your legs in a squat). These
exercises work many muscles at one time and most closely ap-
proximate human movement.

◆◆◆ Move the weight slowly—at least four or five seconds for each
repetition—and through a full range of motion to make strength
gains.

◆◆◆ Engage in active recovery between sets. Instead of doing nothing until you're ready for the next set, stretch or work another body part.

◆◆◆ Don't neglect your cardiorespiratory workouts. Many athletes do cardio workouts on days when they don't train with weights. In many cases, your main sport (in-line skating, biking, and so on) will provide the cardio workout.

◆◆◆ Be consistent. You can realize great benefits by weight training as little as twice a week, as long as you do it every week.

Note: These are general tips. A certified personal trainer can help you design a weight training program with sport-specific goals.

Cross-Training Outside the Gym

Effective cross-training reinforces muscle memory needed in the athlete's primary sport. It can also build strength, flexibility, and/or endurance in a way that's complementary to the athlete's main sport, giving the athlete better muscle balance. The activities extreme athletes have relied on for cross-training range from standard programs like tai chi and yoga to techniques they've discovered themselves. Most of them have broad applicability to people outside extreme sports as well, because they emphasize fundamental competencies like good balance, quick reflexes, coordination, and flexibility.

Pistol Pete Loncarevich, called the "#1 greatest BMXer of all time" by *BMXer* magazine, works out in the dojo. He is one of many competitors who feel the ancient disciplines of the martial arts support their sport-specific training by fine-tuning their balance, timing, and thinking process. Pete even got so good at a Brazilian jujitsu called Gracie jiujitsu, in fact, that he took silver in the Pan American Championships in 1995 and was the American international jujitsu champion in 1998.

And where would Olympic gold medal skier Jonny Moseley be without his years in the ballet studio?

> I had six years of dance, including four years of ballet. I started ballet at ten or eleven—I did it for skiing. It was my dad's idea. My dad always thought it would help out my sports. Then when I got into more modern, social dancing, I started to actually like it. It's not that I didn't like ballet, but I was always the only guy. At first, I thought it sucked. Then at fourteen or fifteen, I thought, "Hey!" My friends started getting into it. They thought, this is too easy—surrounded by hot girls all day.

Jonny also studied gymnastics, which, like dance, cultivates a 3-D body knowledge and flexibility that are applicable in many other environments. Sometimes, that in itself is enough of a risk-mitigator. Even without having done the particular stunt or sport before, the athlete's body knows how to move and protect itself.

Other training techniques and tools top athletes use include:

◆◆◆ Hula Hoop. (If you don't know what it is, ask mom.) Jamie Simon, who is a certified massage therapist in addition to being a champion play boater, says it aids lower-back flexibility—essential for executing an Eskimo roll, which involves a hip snap to right the kayak after capsizing.

◆◆◆ Balance board. Surfers, skateboarders, and snowboarders use it to improve balance. For the same reason, it would be useful to anyone who needs to work on balance, whether it's to improve diving from the high board or bowling. The 1970s bongo board is the precursor of this training device, which has a roller or wheel centered on a short, contoured board.

◆◆◆ Spinning bike. Carolyn Curl uses this stationary bike to work her legs for speed skiing and mountain biking when Portland's weather is too wet, which is often. Spinning bikes have a tension knob that allows easy simulation of riding on hills of all sizes as well as flat roads. Generally, spinning instructors guide classes through elaborate fantasies of mountain rides and vicious dogs at the riders' heels.

◆◆◆ Running on soft sand. The way she runs, Cathy Sassin creates dual benefits of endurance training for adventure racing and team building:

When I go running with someone on the sand here in Santa Monica, there's a bike path right next to us. If I'm running at a pace that I'm happy with and they can't keep up, they can jump on the bike path and it's easier and we can run together. Or if I'm running with someone who is faster, they can wear a weight vest, carry a water bottle, or do something that will make it more difficult for them so we run at the same pace. So we're constantly adjusting to make both of us feel the same, do the same work, accomplish the same thing.

◆◆◆ Pilates. Josef Pilates originally developed this method of body work in the early 1900s and used it to help dancers improve their flexibility, muscle balance, and coordination. Many athletes as well as nonathletes have been introduced to it as part of a rehabilitation program after an injury; it keeps them exercising, strengthening supporting muscles, without actually involving the injured area. Usually, Pilates involves specialized machines and a certified therapist or trainer.

◆◆◆ Slack lining, or loose rope walking. Dean Potter, the first person to free solo (no ropes) three quarters of the way of the northwest face of the 8,836-foot Half Dome in Yosemite National Park, uses this technique to train himself to confront his fear and improve his balance. "Slackers" walk across a nylon rope, usually while tethered to it by a leash attached to a seat harness. Unlike tightrope walkers who carry a pole to help with balance, "slackers use only their arms in a tai-chi-like movement, with bent knees and a fluid yet slow motion."* It doesn't have to done over a chasm, of course. A rope between two boxes in the backyard will give you the feel of the exercise.

♦♦♦ Yoga. Surfer Jeff Clark starts every day with a yoga workout, which helps him stay flexible, balanced, and centered when he snaps to his feet on his long board and guides it down the face of a thirty-foot wave.

Cross-training techniques like these effectively promote mental and physical advantages because the athletes do them regularly. Just as in weight training, the benefits in performance result from consistency of effort.

> **Identify the major movement patterns of your sport. Explore the ways to train for them without doing the sport itself.**

Some athletes use other sports to cross-train, principally in their off-season. Here is a sampling of the sports and the benefits they yield:

---

*"A Spiritual Quest on a Rope—At 1,200 Feet," *Los Angeles Times,* November 28, 1998, p. 1.

♦♦♦ Stunt biker T. J. Lavin goes for motocross: "The crossover with motocross helps me to sharpen my reflexes."

♦♦♦ Skier Scot Schmidt likes the feel of dirt bikes: "Speed, air, timing, reading the terrain coming at you—it's the same with skiing." He uses the holes and bumps and the turns and banks in making moves; he uses the terrain to give him "the flow."

♦♦♦ Skier Wendy Fisher water-skis and mountain-bikes when she isn't on the slopes. All develop essential strength in the quadriceps and the gluteal region, as well as dynamic balance.

♦♦♦ Street lugers Tom Mason and Biker Sherlock surf, which builds strength in the arms and cultivates the rhythm needed for luge at the start. Both sports require a rapid paddling motion. The twenty-five-foot paddle zone in most short-distance luge competitions makes it imperative that competitors focus on this skill if they want to have any hope of winning.

Cross-training can keep the mind tuned up for the athlete's main sport as well as the body. Franz Weber, the world record speed skier, says: "When you speed ski, you don't get much practice overcoming fear. You only go that fast a few times a year." That's why he has done rock climbing and skydiving, and taken other calculated risks throughout the year—to practice managing fear. He feels it has helped him avoid getting hurt: "Fear—you need to practice getting past it."

Finally, in using other sports to cross-train, there's the fun of doing something different, something challenging that keeps the athlete fit, but isn't associated with the pressure of winning. Jonny Moseley is a prime example of someone who reaps huge benefits from "playing around."

When he showed up at the ABC Superstars event in 1998, the other pro athletes thought they had nothing to worry about. Sure, they thought, he does radical tricks on skis, but chances are he can't golf, swim, bike, Jet Ski, kayak, *and* run an obstacle course. Well he can and he did. His most notable effort was smoking Pittsburgh Steelers quarterback Kordell Stewart, known for his versatility, on the obstacle course. Jonny:

> I don't believe I'm necessarily a natural athlete. I definitely was born with a little bit of talent, but just growing up being open-minded about basically anything athletic has made me be able to be versatile. From team sports to solo, I tried everything, from soccer and baseball to surfing and skiing. That's where my ability to do so many sports well comes from. It's that muscle memory. So when I want to go into a new sport like golf, the coordination is there. All I have to do is learn a little bit and train a little bit. I'm not a great golfer, but I have the mechanics.

Special Training Facilities

To refine a trick or develop a special skill, some skydivers and climbers, for example, occasionally use indoor training facilities. Recently, however, a few skydivers have deviated from that by using a training facility to learn and practice their full range of air skills—from basic flying to sophisticated moves that have won them awards in competition.

How Top Athletes Use the Facilities Steve Verner and Sammy Popov had only forty-nine jumps together prior to taking the silver at the U.S. Nationals in skysurfing and freeflying as the skysurfing team called Double Trouble. Medalists in contests like the Nationals and the X Games typically make 500 to 1,000 jumps a year together in preparation for those competitions, so Steve and Sammy either had a new way of doing things or they were incredibly lucky.

Mary Tortomasi and camera-flyer Dean Ricci had a similar success story as Team Flyaway. Not only was their team jump count low

USING SPECIAL TUNNEL SUITS, SKYSURFER MARY TORTOMASI AND CAM-
ERA-FLYER DEAN RICCI, TEAM FLYAWAY, TRAIN IN THE FLYAWAY WIND
TUNNEL IN LAS VEGAS, NEVADA.

CAMERA-FLYER STEVE VERNER AND SKYSURFER SAMMY POPOV PRACTICE A DIFFICULT GRAB IN THEIR STANDARD SKYDIVING JUMPSUITS. IF THEY FALL OFF THE COLUMN OF AIR, THEY CRASH INTO WELL-PADDED WALLS.

when they took silver at the women's open division at the Nationals, but Mary was a low timer on the board itself. Outperforming people with hundreds of board jumps, she successfully executed advanced moves after roughly 100 jumps.

Both teams trained in an indoor vertical wind tunnel in Las Vegas, Nevada, something that used to be nothing more than a roadside amusement. Dean Ricci explains:

> If you start with the tunnel, you learn body positions without worrying about saving your life. You create a muscle memory. Then you can take a controlled body into the sky and focus on safety without worrying about an out-of-control body in freefall.

In the early 1980s, wind tunnels in Las Vegas and in Pigeon Forge, Tennessee, entertained tourists on their respective strips. (Pigeon Forge is just down the road from Dollywood.) Nonskydivers ran them as amusement facilities that allowed visitors to "fly" on a column of air. When skydiver Gary Speer took over the Pigeon Forge operation in 1984 and the Las Vegas Tunnel in 1995, he turned up the air velocity to 115 miles an hour and transformed them into training centers. Tourists still go there daily, but the modifications he made give skydivers an inexpensive way to simulate free fall. Normally, skydivers get a minute to practice during a single skydive; if it takes fifteen minutes to get good at a new move, that's fifteen jumps. At $17 per person per jump, that's $510. Fifteen minutes of practice for a team in the wind tunnel is $35.

Skysurfers can use a vertical harness that Sammy developed to learn board tricks in the tunnel; freeflyers can also use it to learn their stunts, which involve body angles and rotations not used in conventional-formation skydiving.

The skysurfers' experience in the wind tunnel is analogous to climbers learning and practicing at an indoor climbing wall or on bolted routes outside. They focus purely on developing physical and technical expertise, without any of the save-your-life issues that make the sport high-risk.

Advantages of Doing Extreme Moves in a Safe Place In one sense, this makes such specialized training facilities valuable environments for people curious about exploring the high-risk sports of skydiving and climbing. You can get a taste of the forces of nature while building to a "competence rush." On the other hand, these facilities don't provide experience managing the risks associated with the reality of the activity.

Getting that real-life experience may not be as daunting a challenge when the skills are there, though. If you train inside for outside sports, by the time you actually leave the plane or get on the rock, your muscle memory should enable you to focus effectively on the safety issues at hand while your body performs well technically.

Convinced that gym-trained climbers were behind rising injury statistics, Will Gadd (a professional climber and writer in addition to being a paragliding world record holder) researched his theory for an *Outside* magazine story: "I got all the accidents in North America—I thought this was real. What I discovered in accidents in North America was that it wasn't happening." Climbers who simply pushed too hard caused most of the problems.

The wind tunnel and climbing gym are unusual training devices in that they offer stand-alone experiences. They don't necessarily lead to skydiving or to outdoor climbing adventures. People who want a taste of the extreme without swallowing the risks can do that and athletes who want to leave the risk behind for a day and focus on skills can do that, too.

Electronic Aids

In some sports, simulating the moves is much harder to achieve than the sensation of free fall or the feel of a rock formation. Casey Mears has used a computer game that accurately represents the Vancouver racecourse to give him a good idea of whether or not he would come up on a right- or left-hand curve, whether it would be tight, whether he could stay on the throttle, and so on. It doesn't give him a kinesthetic experience, though. Top-fuel boat driver Jim Faulkerson brings sophisticated engineering skills to his racing, but he says he can't re-create the feeling of racing the boat. Like Casey and the Blue Angels, he handles forces that can't be easily simulated:

> The forces acting on you are orthogonal [at right angles] to your body—relocating the internal organs, primarily in the chest cavity. You feel a pressure on the back of your rib cage, a subtle feeling like your organs are being pushed to your back. The skin tingles as it pulls taut, your eyes go out of focus momentarily because the fluid in them gets smashed down. And it all happens so quickly, it's hard to recognize the individual sensations as they're happening.

So, since athletes going at such high speeds can't yet train by simulating the extreme conditions,* they rely heavily on data acquisition systems on their equipment and on their bodies to record precisely what they experience during a race or full-throttle practice run. That helps them make more sense out of the rapid sequence of events so they can improve their driving performance as well as the performance of their machines in the future.

---

*Something called "force feedback" technology will allow accurate simulations in the very near future.

Telemetry on Gear The computer equipment in Jim's boat, the *Nitro Bullet,* samples at a thousand times a second all of the parameters of the engine and the boat during his sub-six-second run. The system stores the information and allows Jim to closely monitor engine parameters. As long as the engine functions at peak performance, then the primary variable in winning is Jim's timing in throwing the throttle at the start.

Casey's on-board telemetry records data on suspension travel, G loads, throttle position, steering input, and more. The Mears crew downloads the data from both Casey's and his cousin and teammate Clint's computer systems after races or practice sessions, then compare the information to improve team performance. They split the track into sections and see which driver went faster on a particular corner. If Casey's faster on one and Clint is faster on another, they can hone each other's technique to go faster as a team. Information like this is also critical to get an edge in Indy Light racing, which emphasizes team preparation and driver skill through the use of identical race cars.

In nonmotorized sports, since the focus is not on engine performance, telemetry is used to monitor elements such as suspension geometry and dynamics of suspension. Pete Loncarevich firmly believes in the performance advantages telemetry gives him. After leaving the BMX world as a Hall of Famer, Pete took his skills into downhill mountain biking and again established himself as a champion.

On a bike, when you're going down a hill, a monitoring device on your suspension can tell how much suspension you're using. It can tell when you're turning whether the angle of your head tube on your bicycle is sufficient for the grade that you're going down. There's a gyro device that maps out the whole course. You can tell where you're dragging your brakes, if you're getting tire slippage or tire grip, etc.—a whole range of problems and conditions.

You can put the computer system on three different riders

CASEY MEARS AND HIS ENGINEER ANALYZE DATA ON CAR AND DRI-
VING PERFORMANCE COLLECTED FROM A PRACTICE RUN AT THE
NAZARETH SPEEDWAY. IT WILL BE USED TO MAKE EXTERNAL AND IN-
TERNAL ADJUSTMENTS IN THE CAR, AS WELL AS HELP CASEY FINE-
TUNE HIS DRIVING ON THE COURSE.

and overlap the results on one display. You can see who rides faster on certain areas of the course and see what the other person's not doing, so the riders can achieve what they want to do—which is win.

You put it all together like a puzzle. Races are won by a tenth of a second, so if you know where you're going and you can make up seconds by letting off the brakes here and there, you can make up a lot at the bottom of the hill, which can make you a champion.

The telemetry helps determine what the bike is doing as well as what the rider is doing. The rider may feel that one thing is happening and tell the engineer, but the engineer relying on the telemetry may find that something else is actually happening. For example, a rider may feel that the bike is diving down at a certain point, but the telemetry may indicate that it's level. This likely means that the rider is leaning too far forward. Adding a video camera to the mix of tools gives the complete picture.

Telemetry on the Body More and more athletes are also using telemetry on themselves, not just their gear, to improve contest performance. It is possible to do well on the mountain bike circuit by "just" pedaling, for example—that's how multisport champion Shaun Palmer says he trains—but Pistol Pete is confident that, at some point, improvements don't happen without science. He credits the National Athletic Health Institution in Los Angeles for opening his eyes to this in 1987 by introducing him to the VO_2 max (maximal oxygen consumption)* test. Tests like this and periodic use of a heart-rate monitor equip him with the information he needs to train properly in zones, that is, focus on precise aerobic and anaerobic goals. Some of his workouts are

---

*VO_2 max represents an individual's maximum aerobic capacity. VO_2 is the volume of oxygen consumed.

RIDERS AT CAMP WOODWARD STORM THROUGH THE SUPERCROSS COURSE.

meant to boost his aerobic capacity, for example. Other times, he does anaerobic threshold training to increase the maximum intensity that he can sustain.*

> **At some point, you reach the limits of your natural ability. You can only go further with scientific training.**

The first step to using telemetry to enhance your performance is establishing your baseline measurements. Go through a comprehensive fitness assessment at a well-equipped fitness or physical therapy center to determine your:

- Cardiorespiratory efficiency, both at rest and during exercise
- Heart rate
- Blood pressure
- Muscle strength
- Endurance
- Flexibility
- The percentage of body fat you carry

Some medical and research facilities offer sophisticated and accurate means of determining maximal oxygen uptake and body fat—the latter is conducted with hydrostatic, or underwater, weighing—but don't expect to find them at the local gym. Once your get your baseline numbers, use common tools like wearable heart monitors and the sensors you grip on treadmills and exercise bikes to keep you in touch with your progress as you train for your big event.

*For specific guidance on the four training zones to peak fitness, see Marc Evans, *Endurance Athlete's Edge* (Human Kinetics, 1997).

BIG AIR, HUGE AIR

"Third round of competition. Final round of competition. If they're gonna do it, they're gonna do it this time. We have Jonny Moseley in the lead with Cusson in second and Dorion in third." Announcer Glen Plake, a pioneer freestyle skier with a foot-high magenta mohawk stiff from Niagara Spray Starch, could never prepare the crowd for what was about to come in the first Big Air Contest, X Games 1999.

As the fans waited, Glen took the wax out of their ears: "This stupid voice you're hearing is Glen Plake. Just in case you care. I'm watching a dream come true, man. I've been working really hard to try to make skiing cool, and gosh darn, it finally is! Yeah!" He laughed. It was like a big party that sunny January afternoon in Crested Butte, Colorado. Glen was rolling. Candide Thovex, "a sixteen-year-old yahoo" from Ance, France, was in the gate. Glen gave the crowd a quick tip: "If you ever take a sweetheart to France, take her to Ance and I guarantee you success there." The French yahoo's 720 with a grab amazed everyone and landed him fourth place.

Soon after that, Jean-Francois Cusson of the Canadian Air Force was in the gate.

At the start, before his first run, J.F. had been doing a kind of hop and slither dance with teammate Vincent Dorion, who had executed perfect 1080s—three complete rotations—in training. The impromptu warm-up set them apart from skiers doing leg swings and other ballistic stretches. Jonny "Big Air" Moseley mostly paced and smiled. There were no reporters, no cameras in anyone's face up there. At the top of the windy hill, it was just a handful of worker bees and twenty happy guys ready to hit the slope. One by one, they left the gate and skied to the line where they would set up for a

J. P. AUCLAIR OF QUEBEC HAD FINE MOMENTS, BUT NOT ENOUGH
TO PUSH INTO THE TOP RANKS AT THE PREMIERE BIG AIR CON-
TEST.

A LIMBER J. F. CUSSON OF THE CANADIAN AIR FORCE LOOKED RE-
LAXED AS HE ATTEMPTED TO LAUNCH HIMSELF INTO FIRST PLACE—
BACKWARD—AT THE BIG AIR CONTEST.

jump. With each grab, cross, spin, flip, and glide, all the guys still at the top hooted and yelled for their ski buddies.

The X Games Big Air Contest has its origins in aerials, a freestyle discipline relying on big ramps from which skiers take off into "simple" tricks like spread-eagles (legs spread wide in the air), backscratchers (ski tips drop and tails of the skis touch the back), and helicopters (360 degree spins), as well as complicated flips with twists. In 1994, two years after mogul competitions became an Olympic medal event, aerials joined the Olympic program. The Big Air Contest is essentially aerials on a smaller scale, giving skiers a single ramp and a limited amount of time to perform. A comparable X Games snowboarding event preceded the skiing contest by two years. In both cases, judges for Big Air score the amplitude, difficulty, landing, and fluidity of the attempt on a 1–25 scale, with the maximum number of total points being 100.*

J.F. left the gate for his third run. He threw a fakie-to-fakie 720 degree twist, which means he began and ended it backward.

"This is the greatest jump we have seen here today!" Glen could barely project above the screaming crowd that had just watched a lithe Canuck challenge Jonny for the top spot.

After a few more runs, the crowd saw America's Olympic gold medal hero in the gate. Glen saw a pal. "Up at the top of the hill, Jonny Moseley, a killer guy. An unbelievably awesome, cheap mechanic. Not afraid to get his fingers dirty. Knows how to weld." At that moment, Jonny held the lead by a full two points.

He saw the signal to go. Nothing in Jonny's face or attitude suggested that he had a severely bruised back, sustained when he had crashed into a fence during practice. He was poised, wearing his helmet with a giant third

---

*After this, it becoms extreme math. According to ESPN's official rules, "the high and low scores for each jump will be thrown out and the remaining four scores added together, divided by four and carried to two decimal places to yield the following scores:

Final Round: first jump score
                second jump score
                third jump score
Final Round score: Each competitior's top two scores are added together and divided by two."
The primary method of resolving ties is to take the higher third score.

JONNY MOSELEY MAKES THE GRAB HE HOPES WILL HELP KEEP HIM
IN FIRST PLACE AT THE BIG AIR CONTEST.

eye on the front. (The official word from the booth was, "Three eyes help him land better than two eyes.")

With the sun in his face, Jonny set up for a 720. The crowd shrieked and clanged cowbells. He wound it up, dropped his shoulder, and went for a grab, but had a little trouble. The landing was hard, but he recovered and moved right toward the spectators with a winning smile.

Without a doubt, the largely American crowd remembered Jonny's stunning victory in the Nagano Olympics a year before. They felt tied to him, proud of him, and wanted him to win again. Based on the cheers from the U.S. competitors, even they wanted him to show off his best. Before the start, one of them said, "Jonny won the big one, and we think that's cool."

Jonny doesn't take that admiration for granted.

Anyone who's been at the top knows that the only way to tell how good you really are, and whether you're really a champion, is through the eyes of your peers—the people who do it with you. They know best. People can win World Cups, or Olympics, or Super Bowls and it may have been one of those days they got lucky. They won't have that respect from their peers. The people who really know the sport recognized that person won that day, but he's not really a champion. If you're that person—the person who won—you can feel the burning eyes of your competitors on you, knowing that you won something, but you're really not a champion.

When it came time to mount the podium, Jonny was a step below J.F. and one above Vinnie, but it didn't matter. They're all champions. You couldn't ask for more from a contest.

Conditioning routines will help you reach a certain level of mental and physical readiness to pursue a goal like win a contest or explore the wilderness. But there's a difference between being "in the game" and being a champion—the one who achieves that goal again and again. Learn from the champions how to overcome obstacles and solve last-minute problems to get the result you want.

KIM Csizmazia (pronounced "chizmazia"), now known primarily for her winning streak in ice climbing events, has always maintained a very high level of fitness for competition. She transitioned smoothly from ski racing to mountain bike racing, then kept pursuing new adventures. Even after she took time off from competing, she kept the habit of training hard. So when she returned to competition and entered the 1995 Survival of the Fittest, a multisport televised event, she expected to win. Instead, she got hurt in that contest and took second the following year. Her reaction to getting hurt was "Why?" Her reaction to coming in second was "Why not first?"

"There is no logical reason why I can't win," she reasoned. So many of the activities, like running on

rough terrain and climbing, were things she'd trained to do since child-hood. Her only weak point was the water—or so she thought.

Kim discovered there were mental "tricks" she needed to use just before and during a competition to give her an edge. She realized training hard wasn't good enough to help her claim the top spot in the Survival of the Fittest.

Mind Games of a Winner

First, she identified habits and behavior that undermined her. She saw these things in other people who weren't winning, too:

♦♦♦ Making excuses right before a competition. Athletes broadcast their supposed ailments and troubles: "My hamstrings are sore." "The altitude kept me awake last night." "I'm great on the bike, but lousy in the water."

♦♦♦ Revisiting mistakes while the competition is occurring. In tennis, competitors call it "playing the last shot."

♦♦♦ Anticipating trouble during the event. Focusing on a challenge or problem that might occur, such as swimming in 45 degree water or canoeing through rapids, instead of staying positive and present in the moment.

Once she identified the problems, she knew they all had a flip side and, out of each one, she developed a plan of action:

♦♦♦ Get rid of the excuses.

In the weeks before the contest, she kept writing herself notes about how much she loved white water, loved cold water. She says, "It worked." Her hesitation about the water events eased up.

Deliberately planting a positive message can have astonishing results. I was once scheduled for facial surgery, but did not want to go under anesthesia. The day before, I had a session with a hypnotherapist who gave me post-hypnotic suggestions like "The surgeon's touch is very soothing," and "You'll feel only pleasant sensations—no pain." The hypnotherapist convinced the surgeon to do his job without administering anesthesia, so I was awake during the procedure. I saw the scalpel coming towards me and when the surgeon cut, I felt pressure, but no pain. In fact, when the surgeon asked me if I could also control my bleeding, the bleeding slowed dramatically.

> **To maintain high performance in clutch moments, your mind must be able to feed on supportive thoughts, just as your body must find a source of energy.**

◆◆◆   Keep looking forward, not back, throughout the event.

Kim looked at the big picture. In the Survival of the Fittest, there are seven events, each of which is done twice. They can involve a variety of challenges—with ropes, on water, running on rugged terrain, obstacle courses, and more. It is possible to never come in first in a single event and still win the contest. She let it sink in that, in this contest, there are fourteen different opportunities to excel. Conversely, turning in a performance in one event that was disappointing could mean very little to the final rankings.

Not to get too deep, but the Survival of the Fittest sounds like life—lots of chances to excel, so you don't have to consider yourself a failure if you fall short occasionally.

◆◆◆   Stay positive at all times.

Looks good on paper, right? Kim knew that she would have to focus consciously on this throughout the contest. Being aware of it as a mental goal prior to that certainly helped. And something happened during the race that seemed like an ironic, cosmic affirmation of her "positive thinking."

It rained every day.

I always felt as if I did better on a nice, sunny day—that I didn't do well in bad weather. It would put me in a bad mood. It rained every single day during the contest. It rained so much that the white water where the event was supposed to take place was washed out. There was actually too much water to get on the water. It was a very positive outcome for me that was totally unexpected.

I stayed really positive about everything and had a lot of good-luck incidents, but I also believe now that if you keep really positive about things, it seems that positive things will happen. I like to treat it that way.

> **Positive thinking yields positive results.**
> **It's not a coincidence.**

The story has a happy ending. Kim emerged as the top woman in the 1997 Survival of the Fittest. She has also won just about every other contest she's entered since then, including high-profile ice climbing contests like the 1998 and 1999 Winter X Games and all three climbing events at the Annual Ouray Ice Craft Invitational Exhibition.

AFTER A ROUGH START, KIM CSIZMAZIA KEPT MOVING TO THE TOP
OF THE TOWER TO WIN THE 1999 WINTER X GAMES ICE CLIMBING
CONTEST—HER SECOND CONSECUTIVE WIN.

Event-Specific Training Tips

Some athletes do specialized activities to prepare them for events. These examples illustrate proven techniques, which hopefully will spark your creativity in designing new elements of your own training program:

◆◆◆ In the days before luge competitions, where he has won the gold a number of times, Rat Sult paddles up the hill near his house (one eighth of a mile) every night. Just as Tom Mason and Biker Sherlock boost their paddling skills by surfing (see Chapter 4), Rat builds arm strength and develops paddling rhythm for a powerful start by repeatedly doing his uphill climb. And neighbors enjoy it: "Little kids follow me up, then ride down."

◆◆◆ High-altitude mountaineer and world record skydiver D. D. Bartley devised a routine she now uses before every major climb. "I train very differently for high-altitude climbs from almost everyone else I know. Most everyone I know runs. I pull a sled."

The first time D.D. did her sled-pull regimen was before an Everest climb. For weeks, she hauled a heavy sled daily for two to three miles and at each end of the pull, she did push-ups and sit-ups. As an experiment that first time, she also did it in her bare feet to see if she could build up a tolerance to the cold and toughen her feet. The results of that part of the experiment were only partially encouraging. She still got cold feet, but no blisters. The rest of it, however, was an amazing success.

I was keeping up with Sherpas on the lower part of the mountain. I realized that the sled pulling felt exactly like climbing. You go very slowly on the mountain, so why not train that way with the same type of pressure and breathing? There was so much squeezing on

my chest from the weight and the pull of the sled, it felt just like
climbing a mountain.

◆◆◆ Todd Skinner will forever be remembered for many firsts, but his
first free climb of Trango Tower's East Face affirmed that his training
emphasis on gymnastic sport climbing definitely pays off at high
altitudes. To prepare to free climb the 3,000-foot granite spike, the
top of which reaches 20,469 feet, Todd and his Wyoming cowboy
buddies had trained at indoor and outdoor bouldering gyms. This
approach resulted from trial and error after years on big walls.

"The gymnastic power required in just six feet of climbing has a real
and logical application on a mountain. They are entirely different
things—almost like being different sports—but the power you gain
and the belief in your power that you gain on these boulders and in
the gym doing gymnastic power training inspires confidence when
you see a stretch of rock 3,000 feet off the ground. And physically, if
you can do any six feet of climbing in the world that's free
climbable, then you're not going to be stopped by a moderate or
even a difficult section twenty-five days later."

Himalayan mountaineers thought the free climbers were fools
not to go to the Himalayas to train, because they considered both their
challenges very similar. In reality, they are quite different. Training on location helps mountaineers to be familiar with how the snow forms on
particular ridges and how their bodies will perform on that terrain while
suffering the deleterious effects of high altitude like muscle loss. They are
wading through snow slogging uphill (see D. D. Bartley's description
above), and at high altitude, that's exhausting. It does not, however, require powerful contractions as in free climbing. Todd and his team needed
to retain enough strength to make it all the way up the wall, despite the
steady muscle deterioration caused by the altitude. To have the power to

do the end of the climb, they reasoned, they had to begin with big, big muscle power. Todd maintains that training in the bouldering gyms "was the exact right way to prepare. On Trango, I think that saved us."

Organizing to Beat the Odds

In some activities, the only way for the athlete to prepare adequately for the contest or adventure is to have firsthand knowledge of the site in advance and organize gear, personnel, timing, and other elements around the demands of the site. Sure, it is possible to make a first descent on a wild river by showing up and running it, for example, but why trust luck when you can design your success?

Expedition kayaker Scott Lindgren's first descent of the Thule Bheri ("Big River") in Nepal took three years and two reconnaissance trips to plan. Scott and two friends first ran a portion of it in 1993, just after that area of Nepal was opened to Western tourism, but high water made it impossible to handle more than twenty-five of the river's eighty miles. They had spent three days on a bus and ten days walking into and up the river only to reach a gorge about eight miles long with water flowing at 5,000 cubic feet per second and an average gradient of 250 feet a mile. The average gradient on the river is eighty feet a mile. Their only reasonable option was to put in below the gorge. They knew then that they would have to come back in the hope that the flow in the gorge dropped by a couple thousand cubic feet per second. The following year, they came back in the low season, but without boats. They just wanted to see if the trip was really feasible.

> We weren't convinced it was navigable by kayak. We spent two weeks hiking in and around the whole area and took a helicopter down the main part of the gorge. At that point, we determined that we could undertake one of the most unbelievable trips anywhere.

On the third trip in November of 1995, they flew in by heli-copter, spent a few days at an exotic lake, then hiked down to the river and put in. Five weeks later, they claimed the first descent of the Thule Bheri and had captured the entire thing on film: "It was 100 percent successful. We only portaged four times on the run. Logistically, it was smooth. Artistically, it was a success, too." Scott won an Emmy for cin-ematography for this *Outdoor Life* film, which is part of the *Adventure Quest* series.

Big-wall climbers like Alex Lowe, Todd Skinner, Steph Davis, and Jared Ogden go through a process like Scott's in painstakingly evaluating their challenge. That is, they don't just wander up to a tow-ering slice of granite and slip their fingers into a crack. The climbers camp at the base, sometimes for days, examining the wall with their teams. They use binoculars. They review photographs. They debate with each other about which route to take. They divide it into pitches, or rope lengths; Trango Tower, for example, had thirty-four. Then, after they reach a consensus, they climb. No one who attempts a free climb ascent wants to be 2,500 feet from the base and 500 feet from the summit only to find out that the wall is as flat as plate glass.

Similarly, when professional exhibition skydiver Jim McCormick committed to jumping into Candlestick (3com) Park before a Giants-Cubs game, he knew that any shortcoming in his planning could lead to a dis-aster. The Stick's design and location pose serious hazards to skydivers, which is why resident teams almost never let them jump into events there. Jim knew the ugly possibilities: the notorious and squirrelly winds at the stadium could take him into San Francisco Bay; wrap his canopy around one of the towering light standards above the field; slam him into unoccupied, or worse yet, occupied, seats; dump him on the asphalt in the parking lot; put him on the Jumbotron—literally—or slice him like a piece of cheese on a cable. And, like a climber on a first ascent, he would get no practice. There was no way to simulate this experience, only to minimize the number of variables and prepare for several scenarios. Jim, true to his engineering background, analyzed the myriad possible outcomes and came up with a program to mitigate his risks.

- ◆◆◆ Two weeks prejump: Jim had a parachute rigger modify his canopy so he would be better able to penetrate winds. The "boogie dive loops" modification would allow Jim to angle the front of the parachute more toward the ground, increasing his forward speed and rate of descent.
- ◆◆◆ One week prejump: He went to the stadium to review all the obstacles that needed to be avoided. He brought along another experienced skydiver to get the benefit of a second perspective.
- ◆◆◆ The day before: Jim made four skydives with the banner, jumpsuit, and flotation gear he would be wearing for the exhibition jump. In those practice jumps, he replicated the approach he would have at Candlestick by landing in a tighter pattern than the one he would normally use at a drop zone.
- ◆◆◆ Exactly twenty-four hours before the jump was to occur, he was in a seat at the stadium to gain any insights on conditions: "I wanted to know exactly what was taking place at that hour. There was no certainty it would be the same the next day, but it was potentially useful."
- ◆◆◆ Jump day: Four hours before the event, he arrived at the stadium and thoroughly briefed all ground crew members and provided them with written procedures and a checklist.

He stationed a recovery vessel in San Francisco Bay that would have radio and cellular phone contact with the ground crew as well as with him while he was still in the airplane. Both men on board had advanced life-saving certifications and were professional boat crewmen. (The rough, cold bay has claimed many victims over the years.)

Before leaving the stadium for the airport, he and the ground crew disrupted batting practice by releasing a smoke canister in

THE JUMBOTRON COULD HAVE CAPTURED A NUMBER OF OUTCOMES WHEN JIM
MCCORMICK JUMPED INTO 3COM PARK (AKA CANDLESTICK). THIS WAS THE
BEST.

shallow center field to check on the wind direction and speed.

At the airport, he briefed the pilot, including a review of timing, to be sure that the exit occurred at precisely the right moment. When Air Traffic Control at a major international airport and the National Anthem are involved in timing a jump, there's no room for error.

Because of proximity to the bay, he wore high-quality military flotation gear that could be deployed under canopy if landing in the water was inevitable (because of its weight, skydiving gear creates a substantial drowning risk).

Before he left the aircraft, Jim was in constant radio contact with ground crew about wind conditions above the stadium and on the field. One member of the crew was positioned on the roof of the football press box, the highest point in the stadium, to monitor the winds above the stadium with a digital, handheld wind meter.

As jump time approached, he was over the stadium twenty-five minutes in advance of the jump, having the pilot do practice jump runs (that is, flying the altitude and path he would take for the jump) while he monitored the winds aloft. By the time jump time came, the jump run was precisely where it was intended.

The ground crew released smoke canisters when Jim was visible to give him a sense of ground winds.

Was all this necessary? Yes, most likely his organization and planning averted a bad outcome. On jump day, Jim had slightly stranger conditions to manage than even he had anticipated. In approaching the stadium, he hit an unexpected wall of air that prevented him from penetrating beyond the upper deck. It held him static over the crowd as a soprano sang, "Oh, say can you see. . . ." Finally, thanks to his canopy modifications and maneuvering, he landed as planned in center field. Jim pulled off a rare jump with panache.

Matching Skills and Personalities

As Jim's emphasis on his ground and boat crews implies, the human element in preparation is essential. Is everyone there who should be there to ensure success for the athlete? Is the athlete in the right frame of mind to go forward? Does the team feel like a team?

Jeff Bechtel's presence on Trango Tower as part of Todd Skinner's first ascent team was kismet, a result of Jeff's own persistence and a major blessing, according to Todd. He learned the hard way, by not taking Jeff along in Mali (see Chapter 3), that his friend Steve's younger brother should be on every major expedition he does. Jeff's skill set is invaluable in a big-wall climb.

Steve Bechtel had been plagued by a persistent headache at the base of Trango, so he could not make the attempt. Jeff, who had only been climbing twice before, borrowed his brother's gear to make the ascent.

> He wouldn't stay down! At stages during it, we told him he couldn't come any higher. He shut the radio off and came up. For that particular ascent, because he came up, we were successful—not because he did hard climbing, but because he did everything but the climbing, which one of us would have had to do.

In other words, the skilled climbers took turns leading pitches up the wall and placing hardware in the wall as they went to secure their rope for those below. Jeff wouldn't lead pitches, he would rely on the rope and hardware to help him get up the wall. His being there, however, saved the experienced climbers time and energy preparing food and doing other essential tasks on the wall: "We would not have succeeded if Jeff had not hitchhiked back by himself and come up on the wall and become what he did."

Having had Jeff along on the Trango Tower ascent and having nearly starved to death without him in Mali, Todd decided that Jeff should come to Greenland—not to go up on the wall, but to solve problems.

Todd's team ventured to a giant fjord framed by mile-high walls. None of them had seen anything this dramatic before, even in pictures, and no Americans had climbed there. Slaloming through the ice, they found themselves caught in a fog bank because of "a weird storm factory where the warm currents meet the ice. It creates clouds like magic. In a clear space, these clouds blow out like a magician's trick." Based on the map in his hands, Todd was convinced that the giant tower they sought, Ulamertorsuaq, was in the fog bank.

> Suddenly, the clouds cleared 1,000 feet above where we were staring. In our minds, it should have been sky, but it was still rock. We almost fell off our little boat. We've seen walls everywhere. We've seen walls on every continent. We just weren't prepared for this thing to be so big. It's quite a bit bigger than El Capitan. We were staggered. Took us about thirty-seven rope lengths—a beautiful, fantastic climb. Maybe the best wall we've ever done.

It was so magnificent, in fact, that after the boat dropped them off at the wall, they lost track of how much time they were spending there, and even how many pitches they had done. At one point, they were in one single dihedral (a point where two walls meet in a right-angled inside corner) that was 2,000 feet long: "We'd just get lost." It's no wonder they paid no attention to their fuel level.

> We needed more gasoline, so Jeff just started walking down this fjord. You don't walk in Greenland. You have boats or you don't go anywhere. We didn't have a boat anymore, so he started walking. Almost a week later he came with gas. We knew he would. There was no question when he left. No apprehension, no sense of

whether he'd make it back with gas. We just didn't know when. We knew he wouldn't fail—he couldn't. He came back with gas, riding with an Inuit in a boat.

From now on, Jeff's the first person on every climb I'm doing, then we decide who's climbing. Anybody can climb. Good, technical climbers are so common that you have to sift through them. But people like him who are so tough in the field and so fantastic at coming up with solutions are rare.

Part of being prepared is having the right people to support you. Know what you're not good at, what you personally don't need to do, or what you can't do for yourself.

Skier Wendy Fisher found out in a very dramatic way that the people she needs most to succeed are friends. They help her get into a frame of mind that enables her to peak in competition.

Wendy has to have fun to be at her best. It is not just a peripheral element of her skiing that may or may not happen in competition—it must be there and it took her years to realize that fully. This lesson in precontest preparation came when she was with the U.S. Ski Team and she's proven its value in clutch moments since then.

When she was a sophomore in high school, she made the U.S. Ski Team and loved it—free skiing with friends on the team between runs, goofing around at the start. But eventually her friends got cut and she didn't. Her life turned into a robotic cycle: wake up, eat breakfast, train, look at the forest, take two free ski runs, run the course four or five times, take another free ski run, go inside, eat, sit around, and do it again. By the time she neared the end of her teens, she started having nightmares, was depressed, and begged her coaches to let her take a break. She was dead last in team rankings. She kept asking for time off, but the coaches said no, so she started looking at courses and figuring out where she could fall: "That side hill—I'm just going to lay it over right there and I'll be done."

Admitting, "I could barely ski down the course," Wendy still thought she had to stick it out for her dad. She desperately wanted to make the Olympics for him. One coach who was a friend pulled her aside the night before the Europa Cup and told her to forget it. She would never make the Olympics, so she should go to the Europa Cup and just ski. They talked for three hours. Going into the contest the next day, she knew that only the top three skiers would get to the World Cup. She came in second: "I went from barely qualifying to second because of a talk." From there, she went to the World Cup, where she ranked thirteenth overall.

After leaving the team, Wendy went to college on a ski scholarship in her hometown. Since she was from Incline Village, Nevada, that meant she would be skiing with and against former Olympians; she was not a shoo-in for any of the top positions. Before her first race, she skied a lot with her buddies, but only did one training run.

> On race day, at the start, I ran into an old friend who had been on the U.S. Ski Team with me in the beginning—a pal. We were talking. Suddenly, I was in the gate. I yelled, "See ya, guys!" I was having fun. I had the best run in the past few years. I won the race—both runs were flawless. It was refreshing. I thought, "Oh my God! I don't suck!"

She was right. Wendy has triumphed in movies and contests. To date, she is the only back-to-back winner of the World Extreme Skiing Championships with her 1996 and 1997 victories in Alaska. She's back in the company of friends—that should make anyone feel like a success.

BIKING WITH WOLVES

Before dogsleds hit the Iditarod trail in late winter, Chloë Lanthier-David helps open it for them. She and other backcountry cyclists from around the world compete annually in the Iditabike Extreme, a 320-mile race from Knik to McGrath that goes through the Rainy Pass, the highest part of the Alaska Range. The race is unsupported. Planes don't fly over to make sure the athletes have survived another subzero day. No cell phones. No radios. They are on their own unless they choose to ride with someone else or seek help from people at checkpoints along the route.

We go through the pass, through mountains, gorges, riverbeds, lakes and it's nonstop. We sleep when we think it's safe and we move as much as we can. There's a lot of wildlife there. We can see wolves, moose, and there's a lot out there that we're not even aware is there.

One year, I could see movement from afar. I thought it was a few guys setting up a camp. As I got closer and closer, I saw pairs of eyes and realized it was a group of wolves playing around. Things like that make you start to lose it mentally. You don't know what you're seeing but you know it's real.

It wasn't frightening. I feel really comfortable in the backcountry. I feel I'm in their world. So if I'm relaxed and calm, they'll be intrigued about who I am and what I'm doing there, but they'll leave me alone. There were four to six wolves. They were beside me for a while. Moving, playing.

In the 1998 race in a field of twenty-eight competitors, Chloë biked the course in four days, twenty-three hours, and fifty minutes and earned eighth place. Throughout the race, she rode steadily, sleeping only briefly during the day when the sun was out. She was the only woman, but says that is irrelevant to her and the men: "In what we do, we have to let go of the ego. If they had huge ego, they wouldn't be in this type of racing." She's also short and epileptic. These are also facts, not excuses.

In 1999, Chloë felt charged and prepared to give an even stronger performance. The unknown elements of the race lured and inspired her, but so did memories of the previous year—like the sight of Mount McKinley, or Denali, the highest peak in North America.

> That first night we could see McKinley. I felt relaxed and at peace. I was looking forward to going through the mountains ahead. I remember last year I was surprised: "Oh, my God, Denali is right over there!" It was in my view for a day and a half. I felt so privileged to be able to see that. This year I was looking forward to seeing it.

Just twenty-five miles into the race, competitors faced a mandatory overnight layover at Little Su River. As they bivied comfortably at minus 25 degrees, they expected that to be their last full night's sleep for as much as a week. Conditions that year were far more severe than the year before when the top finishers had managed the course in four days.

When they started the next morning, it was cold and windy, and heavy snow on the trail forced them to dismount their bikes often. At one point, Chloë was not able to ride her bike for twenty hours. She had to walk it forty miles nonstop through rivers and big bush on the path toward the mountains.

> It was windy and cold and I did that partly during the day and finished at night. I knew the checkpoint was fairly close and it was five in the morning. My eyes were closing and I was starting to lose it. My pace was slowing down and I came around a corner hoping to see the checkpoint and it was another leg. So I decided to bivy. I didn't want to because I had been sweating all

day. My body was cold and even through I had a warm bag, it was really cold—about minus 35. I knew if I woke up in two hours, everything was going to be frozen. Well, I woke up two hours later—a lynx was sniffing my sleeping bag—and everything *was* frozen. I couldn't even think of eating because I just wanted to start riding. I did and twenty minutes later, there was the next checkpoint. That's when I found out that the top guy had just left earlier that morning. I got there at 9:30. Mike Curiak, who was sitting in fifth position, had left at nine and the front runner had left at 6:30. I started feeling really competitive and I was extremely motivated. At that checkpoint, I refocused and said, "I'm going for it."

The Alaska Range came next. Chloë started climbing: "I never felt so strong in a race." She stayed on her bike and climbed small ridges where others needed to dismount and walk. When she did walk, small crampons underneath her mid-foot prevented her from sliding back. She had all the tricks of a veteran, including duct tape on her forehead and cheeks to block the wind. Feeling organized and strong, she gave another rider a little help when he flagged. Pushing someone else motivated her even more.

Traveling with Cullen Barker on this leg, Chloë reached the checkpoint at Finger Lake and heard that two friends, Pat Norwil and John Stamstad, had been involved in an avalanche just ahead at Rainy Pass. She asked the person at the checkpoint to radio in and find out about their condition, but communications were poor. She fixed her sights on the Pass to get a first-hand look.

Chloë and Cullen drove each other through the night. When they were nearly at Rainy Pass, he wanted to stop and bivy. Chloë was adamant: "No, no, we have to get there." They joined up with Mike Curiak, a veteran of this and many other endurance races, and rode through fierce winds. Finally, they arrived at the pass ten hours after the near-fatal avalanche that Pat and John had triggered. The scene shocked them.

It was ridiculous to think of going across. The slopes were extremely loaded with snow and the snow contained air pockets. Gently walking started slides. The only reason I would have gone ahead was ego. Finishing this race would mean risking my life. I didn't want to.

Independently, Chloë, Cullen, and Mike arrived at the same depressing decision: they should not go on. In a way, they felt trapped by their backcountry experience. Riders behind them later passed, ignoring the real potential for another avalanche, and nothing happened.

In a way I wish I would have been naive to the danger, but I couldn't. I work in the mountains and it was against my ethics to move forward. It took me ten hours last year to go through that pass. That's half a day being exposed.

It was the best and the worst decision that Chloë could make, but there was comfort in knowing that a total of nine highly experienced riders made the same choice. For them, the odds were poor and racing professionally in the wilderness is not about playing the odds anyway.

What it comes down to is that we have to let go of the ego and the attitude when we're out there. That's why I do these races. If I liked the ego and the pressure and the high life, I'd be doing other races. But my passion is being in the backcountry and the endurance. Going through my highs and lows and making such decisions.

There were two bright spots. Chloë left this race feeling strong for a high-altitude, week-long endurance run in Kenya. She won. She also kept her sights trained on 2000, when she and a few other riders planned to race beyond the 320-mile course and push all the way to Nome on the Iditarod trail—a total of 1,200 miles.

CHLOË LANTHIER-DAVID REDEFINES "ENDURANCE ATHLETE," BUT IT
ISN'T HER NEED TO WIN THAT KEEPS HER IN THE TOP RANKS: "I LOVE
THE BACKCOUNTRY, I LOVE THE MOUNTAINS."

The appropriate gear—not necessarily the latest—can enhance your performance and provide a safety advantage. Learn how to modify gear to meet your needs, when to buy the latest gadgets and clothing, and even when to look back in time for the best tool. You are also invited to see how imagination and technology work together to produce the next generation of high-performance equipment that helps athletes extend the definition of "extreme."

Creating Advantages with Gear

ATHLETES can see measurable performance improvements from a good diet and scientific training, but nothing helps them reset the standards as dramatically as the latest gear. This can have good and bad results.

In 1964 when Ray Darby wrote *The Space Age Sport: Skydiving* he concluded:

> The modern parachute has eliminated almost all the risk formerly associated with jumping. It has taken the jumper out of the classification of reckless daredevil and made him a respected and accepted sportsman, an athlete of sorts in a game that doesn't require great strength or speed.

CHAPTER 6

Except for the first couple of jumps, it doesn't even require a lot of courage.*

He was essentially right for about thirty years.

Unfortunately, gear innovations can also take an extreme sport through a period of trauma before triumph because the capabilities of it outstrip the skills of the users, or are misunderstood by them. This is precisely what happened in skydiving during the late 1990s, when experienced skydivers converted en masse to high-performance, elliptical canopies. Many people made invalid assumptions about the canopy's flight characteristics, and that mistake put some of them in ambulances or body bags. The lesson in that is simple: new gear can be great only if you learn how to use it.

The exciting truth about gear innovations is that new designs and materials do support the evolution of the sports. They make "faster," "higher," and "longer" possible because they either deliver new performance enhancement advantages or new safety advantages. In the case of something like carbon fiber helmets and curved ice axes, they can do both.

The Right Tool for the Conditions

But the latest gear doesn't make a good jock a champion, nor is it always the best choice. In this sense, extreme sports are like carpentry: you want the right tool for the job, not necessarily the newest one.

A classic example of the right tool for the job is the surfboard that Jeff Clark makes just for the big wave that Jeff made famous: the notorious Maverick's off Pillar Point in Half Moon Bay, California. The

---

*Ray Darby, *The Space Age Sport: Skydiving* (Julian Messner), p. 16.

man who admits, "My life is consumed with riding big waves," also says he has made a lifelong study of how a board relates to the water. He has been surfing Maverick's since 1975 as well as big waves in Hawaii and elsewhere and done in-depth comparisons of board performance: "Hawaii boards tend to be flatter and they bounce all over the place at Maverick's." In contrast, Maverick's boards sit in the water in Hawaii a little lower than they do at home in Half Moon Bay—"too much bottom contour for the conditions."

The board-design questions that Jeff asks his customers could be translated into questions that are useful in helping you buy any piece of equipment—boat, bike, skis, or anything fundamental to your sport. Jeff asks:

> What kind of waves do you want to ride? (Instead of waves, you can think slope, surface, and so on.)
> Where will you be surfing (skiing, biking, skating) the most?
> What do you want this board (ski, bike, skate) to do?
> What are you riding (skiing, biking, skating) now and how does it feel?

These sorts of questions also led to the design of a sea kayak that still raises eyebrows. Traditionally, inexperienced paddlers, like most people who rent kayaks at resorts, use boats called sit-on-tops, whereas experienced sea kayakers use cockpit boats. In the latter, the kayaker sits deep in the boat and seals the cockpit with a spray skirt, the bulk of which is worn by the paddler and the end of which attaches snugly to the rim around the cockpit. Not only do experienced paddlers see advantages to the low seating position and skirt, many wouldn't want to be mistaken for a beginner by paddling a sit-on-top once they've squeezed their butts into a cockpit.

When the Tsunami Rangers began playing in surf zones, rock gardens, and sea caves, they realized that being able to get out of the

1992 KAYAK SURFING WORLD CHAMPION DONNA CASEY FLASHES HER WIN-
NING FORM IN A TSUNAMI WHITEWATER KAYAK.

boat in a hurry made a lot of sense. Cockpit boats with skirts don't necessarily allow that. They also wanted more maneuverability than regular sea kayaks, which are designed to go forward. In that respect, they wanted something more like a river kayak. Rangers cofounder Jim Kakuk and his wife, Rebekah, used their common sense and built the first ocean white-water boats—maneuverable sit-on-tops specifically for experienced kayakers who want to play in wild ocean conditions. They use a carbon-Kevlar weave, an aerospace industry innovation, because paddling in those conditions requires a boat with rigidity, not flexibility, as well as something that can take a beating. It also has quick-release seatbelts and hand railings because getting out of the boat fast can be vital, but being able to grab the boat easily and get back in means the fun can resume.

MacGyvering

Sometimes the conditions call for creative problem solving with common materials. The objective is a cheap and easy solution to a performance challenge.

- ◆◆◆ The duct tape that Chloë Lanthier-David strips across her forehead and cheeks helps block the wind and prevent frostbite in the minus 25 degree temperature she feels every day during the week-long Iditabike Extreme in Alaska. She uses it in conjunction with a balaclava when the windchill brings temperatures down to minus 40 or minus 50 degrees.
- ◆◆◆ Some skysurfers wrap their arms in duct tape—this is versatile stuff—for competition because they spin so fast, the blood vessels there would burst without the compression, according to skysurfer Sammy Popov.

BEFORE THE BIKERCROSS FINALS AT THE 1999 WINTER X GAMES, STUDS ON THE BIKE TIRES WERE SANDED DOWN. COMPETITORS WANT TRACTION, BUT NOT SO MUCH THAT IT EATS INTO THE SPEED THEY NEED TO WIN.

♦♦♦ The metal studs that snow mountain bikers have manufacturers put on their tires for the X Games bikercross event give them more grip on the slope. The downside is that, if the studs are too long, they dig into the snow so deeply that they slow the racer down.

♦♦♦ Adventure racers commonly carry thirty-gallon trash bags to stow their packs during water crossings. It helps keep them dry and makes them more flotable. They also have grommets put into their backpack to allow drainage if the pack does get submerged and to provide another place to attach something like a bungee.

♦♦♦ Carolyn Curl always modifies stock boots for speed skiing. She cuts the buckles and puts drag-reducing attachments, or farings, on the back to make them more aerodynamic. They are triangular pieces, usually foam, that come off the calves: "It makes the air flow off your calf more evenly and it doesn't create a vortex there." And even though speed skiers use poles that are bent specially to hug into the body, Curly and others build special baskets on them that are more aerodynamic. She also puts small cones on the ski poles in front of her hands to break the wind as it goes over her hands: "One of the first things the wind hits is your ski poles and your hands. If you can reduce drag at that point you have an advantage."

These types of solutions are what Robert Nagle of Team Eco-Internet calls "MacGyvering." MacGyver, the brainy title character portrayed by Richard Dean Anderson in a popular TV show that ran from 1985 through 1991, rescued victims, vanquished villains, and escaped unharmed by piecing together whatever was handy. Eco-Internet, which includes some academic overachievers, knows that fitness isn't always enough to win an adventure race. They invent things—they MacGyver—as their needs dictate.

Several members of the team are keen on futzing around with little pieces of equipment and figuring out ways of going faster—we don't necessarily look for high-tech answers, but we look around at the materials that we have and cobble together an interesting solution.

They've done it with climbing equipment, kayaks, canoes, and bikes with great success, although race organizers sometimes give them a hard time during the preliminary gear inspection. In the paddling section of the 1998 Raid Gauloise in Ecuador, which they won, they tied the inflatable rafts together with cord, making a semirigid construction. The way they did it didn't merely create a drafting advantage, with the lead boat making it easier for the following boat. They actually made a boat that was twice as long. In paddling, waterline length is a huge contributor to speed of a boat. So their result was a double-length boat they could easily steer down a meandering, winding river. Robert says, "In many sections, we were easily paddling 50 percent faster" than their primary competitors at the time.

Eco-Internet also premiered a towing and pacing system for bikes at the 1996 X Games, then perfected it by the time of the 1996 Eco-Challenge in British Columbia, which they also won. By rigging the bikes together, they enforced a fast pace on good roads and provided a tow for slower bikes on steep hills. A high-strength, low-weight cord attached directly to the seat post of each bike was fed off the back of the bike through the loops on a fishing rod, which was also attached to the bike. The rod wasn't a structural necessity for the system, but it did keep the cord up over the back wheel so it wouldn't bounce over the wheel when not in use. At the end of the cord was a bungee, which looped over a hook on the stem that they put on the handlebars of their mountain bikes. Anyone who was tired during one of the bike legs could reach down, grab the bungee, and slip it over the hook. It attached easily and could be removed in a fraction of a second. Being able to disengage it fast was a critical feature, since it is common to hit a bad patch quickly or unexpectedly in mountain biking.

No one person always leads in the bike legs of the race. The strongest person at the time would lead. Typically, it's the best bikers, but in a race there's no telling who's going to be the weakest at any given time. We set it up so everybody can be towed.

At one of the X Games, the rules stipulated that team members had to use canoe paddles instead of kayak paddles, so they tied them together to make one kayak paddle. It's a lot faster. They won that, too.

Sometimes the urge to invent can backfire, though, if all contingencies haven't been explored. During the 1995 Eco-Challenge, Team Hissardut Survival wore custom-designed backpacks that resembled vests, which worked well during hiking, biking, and the rope course, but weighted them down when wet. As a result, one of the team members suffered a borderline case of hypothermia in the eighteen-mile canyoneering stretch.

Trying to emulate superstars by copying their gear can also produce mixed results. Luger Michael Shannon says, "A lot of the guys getting into the sport videotape the X Games, then play the tape over and over. They build their boards by putting the tape on pause and duping the best ones." For most of them, that means they have a board without the technique to ride it anywhere except into a hay bale.

Before you invent a solution to a problem or buy new gear, ask yourself:

••• What do you *like* about your current gear?
••• What's the specific performance or safety challenge your current gear does not meet?
••• Where will you use this piece of gear the most?
••• Is there any downside to using this gear?

Borrowing from the Past

Some athletes have found their problem solving takes them back in time. That was certainly the case in the 1980s, when short skis were the rage. People knew that long skis worked better in powder, but they were hard to find in the stores; skiers had to pull them out of the attic. Looking backward has also worked in skydiving a couple of times.

BASE (building, antenna, span, and earth) jumpers use basically the same equipment as skydivers, but the risks can be quite different because their sport is jumping off fixed objects. For a particular jump, they might want the flight characteristics of an old parachute that drops them almost straight down, rather than a more modern parachute that has a lot of forward movement. Or they might want to use old gear because it isn't valuable. They might leap off a 900-foot bridge, deploy their parachutes immediately, and deliberately land in a river. They plan for and think through that scenario, which involves using old gear they can afford to ruin. Normally, skydivers only land in water if they have no other option; they don't want to damage new equipment that's worth $4,000 or $5,000.

Freeflying is a more recent variation of skydiving that also got athletes to look back.

When Olav Zipser began exploring new approaches to human flight in 1987, most other skydivers were moving toward tight jumpsuits with spandex panels. Their objective was to reduce drag and set a fast fall rate for formation flying; a fast fall rate translated into more control for the skydivers creating formations. With their belly-to-earth body configuration, a fast fall rate would be around 120 miles an hour. In contrast to them, Olav's head-down flight position, foot-down position, and multirotations gave him a fallrate of 180 miles an hour to almost 300 miles an hour; tight suits worked against him in creating dolphinlike moves. Olav and his freeflying followers went retro: they pulled old, baggy, poly-cotton suits out of storage, renamed them clown

WITH THE INTRODUCTION OF FREEFLYING TO DROP ZONES IN THE EARLY 1990S, BAGGY JUMPSUITS THAT HAD SAT IN THE CLOSET FOR A DECADE ONCE AGAIN FOUND THEIR WAY TO THE SKIES.

suits, and still use them with great success to produce the drag they want as they create three-dimensional formations.

> **Use the gear that works best,**
> **even if it's your mother's.**

Borrowing from Other Sports

Frequently, as extreme sports have emerged and developed, they have also coopted gear from other sports. Curly set the women's world record in both speed skiing and downhill biking wearing a red rubber suit designed for speed skiing. The rubber, turtleneck suit has one zipper in the front at the chest area and putting it on is a chore. According to Curly, "When the suits are brand new, it can take forty-five minutes and two extra people to get into them." She also has worn the same aerodynamic helmet—"not built for safety"—for both sports. The bullet-shaped covering is built to go around the athlete's shoulders and over the face; there is a built-in visor but it doesn't lift up: "Once you get that thing on, it's like being inside Darth Vader's helmet."

Downhill mountain bike racers and kayakers who play in rock gardens often give their shoulders and torsos extra protection with lighter, more maneuverable versions of motocross body armor. And lugers borrowed the concept for their leathers from motorcycle riders.

In the early days of competition, lugers wore unmodified motorcycle leathers, which worked well except that they're lying down so they don't really want pants that are made for someone in a sitting position. The padding in standard leathers is also in the wrong place for a luger, who may slide a long way on his or her rear end after coming off the board at sixty miles an hour.

The need for leathers with padding in the right places was obvious in San Francisco on November 7, 1998, as street lugers blasted down the same steep stretch of Taylor Street where Steve McQueen, as Lieutenant Bullitt, had chased the killer with a Winchester pump in his Shelby Mustang. That Saturday morning, rain made the half-mile stretch of asphalt stair steps even more hazardous than usual: Taylor was slick as it met Green, then headed down steeply toward Union, Filbert, Greenwich, and Lombard. At sixty miles an hour on a luge, it could be a high-speed route to the back end of an ambulance.

Twenty-four of the world's top street lugers had accepted organizer Tom Mason's ("the bad boy of street luge," according to announcer and luge pro Biker Sherlock) invitation to run the hill despite the wet weather. Even under blue skies, the 1998 Red Bull Streets of San Francisco Street Luge Race would have set a precedent. This was the first time a street luge competition had been run on a straight stairstep course that tempted riders to catch air at the cross streets. Racers like Rat Sult called it a "big balls contest."

By afternoon, they got lucky. The rain stopped and a brisk wind helped dry much of the short course.

Waldo Autry, a middle-aged luge pioneer and Skateboarding Hall of Famer, caught air at Filbert and lost control. His body bounced off his gear, slammed onto the street, and slid. A Huntington Beach hairstylist with green stripes through his blonde buzz-cut, Waldo's head matched his leathers. After the fall, it also matched the roughly seventy-foot stripe his rear end left on Taylor Street. Waldo got up and laughed as he walked away. That's what leathers are for.

MERCEDES GONZALEZ, NINE-TIME WOMEN'S MOTOCROSS CHAMPION,
SUITS UP IN HER BODY ARMOR FOR DOWNHILL MOUNTAIN BIKE RAC-
ING WITH TEAM GT.

WALDO AUTRY, WITH GREEN AND YELLOW LEATHERS TO MATCH HIS HAIR, FLIES OFF THIS LUGE AFTER CATCHING BIG AIR ON TAYLOR STREET IN SAN FRANCISCO. HE WALKED AWAY LAUGHING.

Custom-Designing a Competitive Edge

Since catching air is not something lugers normally do, standard boards were not ideally suited to the San Francisco challenge— Waldo's slide proved it dramatically. Jarret Ewanek knew that, so he considered his invitation to the race an opportunity to test his design expertise.

By training, Jarret is an aerospace engineer, but more people know him as Dr. GoFast, the professional downhill racer who specializes in speedboarding and street luge.

> When I first became aware of the race, I was familiar with Taylor Street from a past visit to San Francisco. I knew there would be ledges and had suspicions that the vehicles would be weightless coming off the ledges, if not catching actual air, which is something that was never experienced in luge racing. Knowing the structural limits of the luges, as well as the physical limitations of the human body, I was curious to see what this kind of punishment would do to both.

He took his curiosity to his computer and started running simulations. He accessed Geological Survey maps and targeted the specific points along Taylor Street that marked the start and finish of the race. With that data, he could use his computer-aided design system to build the full contour of the racecourse in one-to-one scale. He then took that model of the hill and put it into sophisticated software called Working Model that allowed him to do mechanical simulations. He used it to see precisely how different mechanical parts would move in relation to each other on the hill.

Using that software, he took a virtual ride down the Taylor Street course. And Jarret saw that running the race with his current luge was a bad idea: with his current luge he would catch a lot of airtime off the hills. He also noticed, and measured, the incredible dynamic and static forces affecting the luge and the components. The software allowed him to predict the path of motion including the flight path of the luge as it was in the air, whether it would pitch or roll, the height in the air, and the distance in the air.

> The force numbers were really, really high. I scratched my head and decided I had to come up with something that would not only make this safer but also give me a competitive advantage. I had a feeling that the other competitors would be tapping the brakes before they were going off the ledge after they experienced the ledge for the first time. My concept was that, if I could come up with a luge that would allow me to hit the jumps without tapping the brakes, a win would be a slam dunk.

Was he right? Jarret made a series of virtual prototypes on the computer and went back to the virtual hill to test them. He went through several iterations until he was satisfied. Finally, he created the drawings for a new luge with full rear suspension and went to his small machine shop and made the parts. By that time, the race was imminent, so he had no time to do any physical, real-world testing. He had to rely strictly on the data he got from the working model and trust his ability to machine the parts as designed.

Six hours before he had to catch his plane, he secured the last set of bolts on the luge. The following morning, during the first practice run on Taylor Street, was the first time the luge ever saw pavement. It was completely unproven and untested—except on the computer.

> At the end of the first run, I was absolutely stoked at how it worked. I was able to hit the bumps very fast. The landings were gentle, exactly as I predicted. The second practice run, I went balls out—no brakes—and I discovered that the passing strategy on this was not on the course, but in the air.

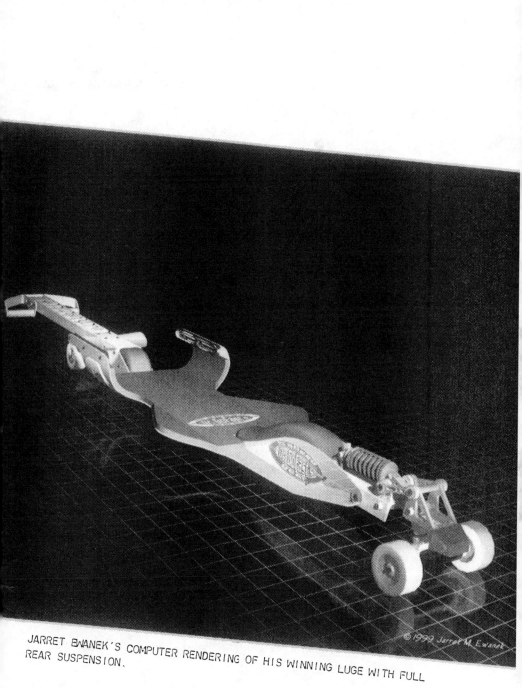

JARRET EWANEK'S COMPUTER RENDERING OF HIS WINNING LUGE WITH FULL
REAR SUSPENSION.

He passed another competitor by going right over him and sped to victory. So, yes, he was right.

I have to attribute it all to the design. It definitely isn't my riding talent. I'm not the most talented rider out there and I make no claims to that. What I do pride myself on is using my technology as my advantage—my so-called unfair advantage.

> ## Your brain can be your best competitive advantage. No matter what you do.

Drawing from any part of you, like life experience, intuition, college physics, personal training, your passion to succeed, your keen reconnaissance—any part of you—cannot be considered an unfair advantage. Whether it's Team Eco-Internet's McGyvering, Chloë Lanthier-David's creative use of duct tape, or Dr. GoFast's redesign of his luge, the ability to think through a challenge is the mark of a true winner.

Jim Faulkerson, a top-fuel boat racer, has followed this impulse since he was a little kid, and now is attempting to redefine the limits of his sport through his engineering acumen.

Jim has built his own machines ever since he was six years old, when he and his father made a small go-cart out of a lawnmower engine, four wheels, and a V-belt connecting the engine to the wheels: "I went fourteen miles an hour at the age of six." Now he builds boats running on nitromethane that go from dead still to 217 in 5.7 seconds—and he's getting faster.

When Jim's fascination with fast boats first surfaced in the 1980s, "engines went from 2,500 horsepower up to almost 4,000 overnight . . . you had a one-in-three chance of dying." The death and injury toll in top-fuel racing remained so high for several years that, at one point, there were only two boats left in the circuit. Insurance coverage was discontinued. He watched what was killing and maiming the pilots and saw a design challenge related both to safety and the ability to set a new world record.

Even now, most top-fuel boats are single-propeller hydroplanes (one propeller turning to provide thrust), which require rapid corrections in power and steering during their short run. Top drivers are highly adept at manipulating the throttle and rudders. They have to squeeze the throttle enough to snap the propeller loose and get the engine revving high enough, roll the throttle just as the propeller starts to hook up to the water, then put enough rudder into it to keep the boat going straight. The propeller is trying to move the boat forward, but the propeller blade turning in the water creates a torque: it tries to take the boat and twist it around the propeller. The result is that some boats do come out of the water and roll at the starting line. Jim says that handling a boat like this "requires very quick reactions, it's very difficult." He thought it was too difficult, in fact, and fraught with danger.

To make the boat more predictable and easy to handle, he developed a hydroplane with a twin, counterrotating propeller system: "Twins have been around since the beginning of propulsion, but not in this sport." Other racers felt strongly that it could not be competitive and the sanctioning body wasn't sure this experimental boat would be safe (safe being a relative term). His *Nitro Bullet* went through eight months of scrutiny in an attempt to get a license to compete on the circuit. The testing process consisted of three elements:

1. No one had ever seen a drive system like this on a top-fuel boat, so he had to prove it was safe.
2. He had to prove he could control it at speeds exceeding 200 miles an hour.
3. Three consecutive times, he had to demonstrate that he had the

presence of mind and the appropriate gear to escape underwater in case of an emergency. For that, they put him in a capsule, pushed him in the water face down so he would have to use his air system, then went through simulated rescues.

For explosions and mechanical failures that were likely to happen, Jim constructed the boat with a pod, a steel cage built to withstand enormous impact, which wraps around his body and over his head. On top of that is Kevlar, a tough, fire-resistant material, and plexiglass. It's actually recycled F-14 windshields that he buys from the government and adapts to the boat. These windshields must be safe, he says, because the government tested them by shooting frozen chickens out of a cannon at them. The pod has control cables going in and out that are set up with yield lengths, so they are designed to break at a certain point and release the cage. It floats and has its own environmental system—compressed air, like a scuba system—to make a crash survivable.

Jim finally got his license. He and the new boat made their first race in June 1997, but not without problems. Two seconds into his run, he had a mechanical failure that took him out of the lineup. Maybe he was better off.

I watched two guys barrel-roll at 200-plus miles an hour—in one case, an air bottle broke loose inside and beat him to death. Having a loose component was a fatal mistake. In the other case, the fellow went in backward—the boat actually barrel-rolled, turned in the air, and went in backward. That caused a structural failure, so when the water rushed in, it snapped his neck. He went into a coma, then died.

There were six boats that day. Within a period of an hour and a half, four boats crashed. It was the blackest day in drag boat racing. June of 1997—six boats running, four accidents, two dead.

There are guys who barrel-roll at that speed and survive. These guys didn't. Being one that survives doesn't make you less afraid necessarily. Watching the guys who didn't can make you more afraid.

Jim didn't like that fear, so he tweaked his boat and went back to the circuit with an improved *Nitro Bullet* that took him to fifth place worldwide in three races: "In *Nitro Bullet,* snap the throttle and you go. It doesn't have the requirements on the driver that a single-prop boat does, so it's easier to repeat the success."

His next step: modifying the design again with lighter materials and a 6,000 horsepower engine—an increase of 1,000 horsepower—for a world record attempt to travel the quarter-mile racecourse in under five seconds.

Future Gear

As stated at the beginning of this chapter, nothing helps athletes reset performance standards as dramatically as the latest gear. Jim and Jarret are proving that with their designs for their personal equipment in dragboat racing and street luge, respectively, and we can expect to see similar advances for all athletes in biking, boating, and many other activities. Soon after that, the advances make higher performance gear available to the rest of us.

Aaron Bethlenfalvy, senior industrial designer with GT Bicycles, says the conceptual and manufacturing work they're doing in the GT shop offers a taste of the future in many sports. At first, the process of creating a new bike appears low-tech: an athlete expresses a problem with the equipment and discusses ways to alleviate it with the design team. The designers then develop conceptual sketches of a solution, see what the athlete thinks of their work, then refine their sketches. Next,

A PROTOTYPE BIKE FRAME MODELED IN FOAM RESTS ON THE FULL-SIZE
PRINTOUT OF THE DESIGNER'S COMPUTER RENDERING IN GT'S DESIGN
SHOP.

TYPICALLY, A LASER MACHINE MITERS THE BIKE'S TUBES VERY PRECISELY, BUT GT HAD TO RESORT TO LOW-TECH HAND-WELDING TO MEET THE TWO-WEEK DEADLINE ON BUILDING CUSTOMIZED BIKES FOR THE TOUR DE FRANCE'S TEAM LOTTO MOBISTAR. EVERY ONE OF THE FORTY-FIVE TUBES NEEDED FOR THE TEAM HAD AN ATHLETE'S NAME WRITTEN ON IT, SINCE THEY WERE CUT EXACTLY FOR THAT RIDER.

they go to the model shop and sculpt a version of the new concept in foam so the athlete has a 3-D sense of the design. They make more refinements, then the engineers take over and generate prints with precise dimensions, wall thicknesses, tube specifications, and other details the frame needs on it for production. That print goes to the fabrication shop, which makes a fully functional prototype that the athlete tests.

Behind the scenes, the process seems more high-tech. Before the athlete tests the bike, the engineers improve their model using software to do fictitious loading on parts of the bike, just like Jarret did with his luge model. They determine points of high stress concentration, where cracks will develop, and so on.

The futuristic aspect of the process relates to new materials and miniaturized onboard computers. Aaron sees carbon fiber as offering many untapped opportunities for bike design: "Not only is it lightweight and strong, it also allows us to be creative with the *form* of the bike." This is because carbon fiber, charred fiberglass mixed with a resin to give it the desired rigidity, can be molded into any shape. It can also be layered. High stress points can have more material than other areas to produce the ideal result in terms of weight and strength. The latest skydiving helmets, ice axes, and many other extreme sports tools are made out of carbon fiber.

Integrating electronic devices will lead to a host of radical upgrades from automatic transmissions to real-time changes in the geometry of the bike. When you go downhill, the angles of the bike would adjust, and when you reach a flat road, the angles would change again to give a more relaxed configuration.

Advancements like this will not only extend performance possibilities for extreme athletes, but also bring more people into the sports on some level. For example, bikes that make automatic, real-time adjustments based on conditions will make it a little safer for people other than extreme downhillers to experience the intense thrill of charging down a 70 degree slope like Ira's Trail, where Team GT members test their nerve, as well as their bikes.

WORLD CHAMPION DOWNHILLER STEVE PEAT OF TEAM GT BLASTS DOWN
IRA'S TRAIL. WHAT YOU DON'T SEE IS THE STEEP CLIFF JUST TO
THE LEFT OF THE TRAIL OR THE SHARP RIGHT TURN AT THE BASE.

ICE CLIMBING FOR GOLD

A man-made frozen waterfall, contoured to have odd angles, loomed fifty feet above the crowd in Crested Butte, Colorado. Near the top, a radical overhang with handholds—plastic disguised as rock—converted the ice tower into a mixed climb.

Mother Nature has very little do to with this kind of waterfall. The underlying structure is a three-sided frame wrapped in steel mesh curtains. The designers spray and drip water over the curtains from nozzles they adjust to different angles and rates of output. By pumping liquid nitrogen into the enclosed space inside the tower, they create a super-chilled environment causing the water to freeze on contact with the mesh. The eventual result is an eighteen-inch-thick wall of ice replete with the bulges and icicles often seen on frozen waterfalls.

The men's event must be completed in eleven minutes; women get twelve. Whoever goes highest wins. If there is a tie, then the least number of sticks, or strikes with the ice axe, decides the contest.

What's so extreme about this? Competitors don't even have to place ice screws as fall protection. All they have to do is hook their belay rope into carabiners on the wall as they ascend. From an old-school climber's point of view, the 1999 X Games ice climbing event may have looked made for gym-trained climbers who have spent a few days outside swinging axes at fat ice.

First, all the facts weren't obvious and, second, looks can be deceiving. Climbers stayed in isolation before their attempt so they could not examine the wall or watch other competitors. They had to leave the trailer with their ice axes, head to the tower, and start. In the wilderness, climbers scru-

JARED OGDEN DOES A FIGURE-4 NEAR THE OVERHANG TO GIVE HIMSELF LEVERAGE FOR A PUSH TO THE TOP OF THE TOWER.

HELGI CHRISTENSEN POWERED UP TO THE OVERHANG, BUT COULDN'T
FIND A FOOTHOLD. AFTER THREE INTENSE MINUTES OF TRYING—
DANGLING FROM ONE ICE AXE, THEN ANOTHER—HE LOST THE BATTLE,
BUT WON THE CROWD.

tinize the ice, pick a line, then go. And this man-made climbing challenge was more extreme than the vertical water ice pitches often seen in nature.

In short, the contest was not an event for low-timers, or an ego stroke for kids who trained hard on a secret crag in Minnesota. This is one reason why it drew a dozen world leaders in ice climbing. They included thirty-one-year-old Calgary resident Raphael Slawinski, who has put up some of the hardest routes in Canada's wilderness, and the Korean expert Seung-Kwon Chung, a veteran of Everest's west side. Gary Ryan and Stevie Haston held up the Brits' honor. Gary has been ice climbing for more than twenty years. He is the talent behind a high-quality, beautiful line called Bladerunner in Rocky Mountain National Park. At forty-one, Stevie was the old man of the group and a pioneer of mixed climbing. Jared Ogden's much younger face had just made the pages of *National Geographic* (with grand masters Alex Lowe and Greg Child) for a first ascent of Great Sail Peak, a 3,750-foot granite wall on Baffin Island. He had won this X Games event two years before. Then there was Will Gadd, one of the top athletes in the world in paragliding and river kayaking, as well as ice climbing (see "Lessons in Action: Paragliding into Guinness"). In Iceland the year before, Will had put up the hardest ice route in the world, the first one to be rated M10. The year before that, it was the first M9, with a lot of nearly comparable routes in the months and years before. He's put up more routes in those grades than anyone else.

In short, the X Games competition was a showcase of the kind of athleticism and logical thinking that ice climbing in nature demands for survival.

The men's event in 1999 began with a climber who could not meet the challenge of the overhang. Then Raphael Slawinski looked at the wall for the first time. At six feet and 160 pounds, his build was similar to that of most of the other climbers. He blasted up the wall, heading to the left of the overhang. Spectators knew it was not the ideal route laid in by the tower's designers. With the athletes in isolation prior to the event, however, there is no way they would know such facts about the climb.

He surveyed the plastic panel with the handholds, leaned back into his crampons, and, hanging from his ice axes, swayed back and forth. Then he took a gymnastic move to the left and "dry-tooled"—used his ice axes on the handholds—toward the ice crowning the tower. At the icicles, he sunk his ice axe and it held steady. The power of his arms helped tremendously as he spent seconds dangling from his ice axes with no foothold. He soon made it to the top. His earned height was forty-nine feet, strike count 41.

One after the other, good and great climbers dug their crampons and axes in the ice, then rested as they stared at the overhang. The route was hard. The ice was brittle. One after another, they fell off the wall before getting a clean shot at the ice near the roof.

The crowd was attentive but not wild until Helgi Christensen from Finland stretched up to the ice slab above the overhang. Could he challenge Raphael's supremacy?

Helgi got a stick, but no foothold. Dangling on one ice axe, he looked helpless. Then with a great swing, he dug his other axe into the ice. Now he was dangling by two axes. At times, he tried powering into a figure-4, a move to gain leverage in which a leg crosses up and over the arm. Still no foothold. As he held for more than a minute, the crowd tried to lift him higher with cheers of "Go! Go! Go!" and clanging cowbells.

He struggled, trying to find a foothold, for *three minutes* before his arms gave out and he swung free of the wall. His belayer, being completely occupied, was the only one who didn't applaud the champion effort. As Helgi walked away from the ice tower, a reporter extended his hand. Helgi, clutching his arms and pumped to the maximum, smiled and apologized: "I don't have the energy."

For the crowd, it was the highlight of the event. Helgi's performance showed why ice climbing is an extreme sport. His strength and tenacity illustrated the ability he has applied to putting in stunning new routes.

Another great moment was still ahead, though. Will Gadd was up. Another thirty-one-year-old Canadian who is six feet tall and 160 pounds, "the Gaddfly" had already earned three golds in previous X Games ice climbing events. One stick after the other, he showed the confidence of a winner; his moves were clean. When he got to the overhang, he yanked his gloves off one by one with his teeth. When he hit the top of the tower—only the second man to do that—he backed away from the wall. His work was done. As Will swung toward the crowd on the rope, he beamed and raised his curved axes in the air. His mantra during the climb had been, "Be organized, be comfortable," and he was.

Having reached a height of forty-nine feet, Will was certain the decid-

WILL GADD POWERS UP TO THE ICE CURTAIN LEADING TO VICTORY.

ing factor would be who had fewer sticks—he or Raphael? He didn't know. One of the reporters who had counted the sticks told him he bettered his fellow Canadian by three. He whooped.

Say what you will about made-for-TV contests: this was a rare chance to see wilderness heroes show off and have fun together.

Have you ever really thought about why you've gotten hurt and how it's affected you later— emotionally and physically? Extreme athletes have to answer why and how. Their careers and lives depend on them improving both their situational awareness and self-awareness. Their lessons will help you do the same.

EVERYONE gets hurt for the same reasons. You break your arm for the same reason an extreme athlete does—you lose focus, someone hits you, and so on— although you may be doing something more conventional at the time. So what can extreme athletes tell you about preventing injuries? A lot. Repeatedly doing a high-risk activity leads to injury at some point. As a result, extreme athletes become aware of how to reduce the chances of it happening and deal with it effectively when it's imminent. They also have valuable insights about managing pain and moving past emotional trauma after an injury.

There are at least five reasons why people get hurt: random accidents, tunnel vision, ignoring that

CHAPTER

sixth sense when it signals trouble, poor judgment, and overconfidence.

Random Accidents

Even fine-tuned situational awareness can't avert a random accident. In this context, accident means a problem that may have been preventable by someone other than the athlete, but it was out of the athlete's control. It's the kind of thing that happened to skydiver Dan Brodsky-Chenfeld.

At 11:13 A.M. on April 22, 1992, a De Havilland Twin Otter carrying twenty skydivers and two pilots crashed seconds after takeoff. The seventy-five-mile-an-hour nosedive into a dirt field instantly killed most of the people on board. Six jumpers—those closest to the door—survived the impact because they were hurled forward into the less fortunate people who happened to be up front. Among those surviving were three members of a nationally ranked four-way team.

Dan survived, but with a broken neck. He drifted in and out of consciousness for weeks after the accident, and still has only fragmented memories of the months prior to it. He remembers nothing of the crash itself. His first clear memory afterward is seeing Kristi, now his wife, standing beside him.

> My eyes were wandering around the room trying to make out where I was. I recognized I was in a hospital, with hoses and machines, and lights blinking. Then I remember going to turn my head to look around more and I couldn't turn my head. There was a moment of horror, thinking that I was completely paralyzed. I stopped for a second and took a deep breath, then wiggled my toes and feet and found that I could move everything except my head. I reached up and grabbed bars that were part of the halo brace and realized that

was holding my head still. Then I was almost laughing. I went from being a quadriplegic to just having a brace on my head. I thought, "That's good. That's a huge improvement."

Dan went through multiple surgeries, but his confidence in his body supported a blistering pace for his recovery. He had a goal to sky-dive again—not just sometime, but in the national competition coming up the following October, six months after the accident.

In July, after the final surgery, his doctor made an official rec-ommendation: "You can't jump ever again." Dan baited him: "There are no lawyers here. I'm not gonna sue you over this. When can I jump?" The doctor was evasive each time Dan posed the question. Finally, Dan challenged him: "Let's get specific here. How long will it take for the actual vertebrae that you're fusing to be strong enough that I won't break it there?" The doctor told him eight weeks.

Eight weeks to the day I was up in the airplane watching my team train. I was considering jumping. They went out and I just had to go. So I bowed out after them. It felt just great—like being released from a cage.

With Dan competing in some rounds, and another teammate filling in on others, Dan's team took third in the national four-way com-petition that year. Since then, they've earned gold repeatedly in na-tional and international meets. To Dan, the accident was just that—an accident. It has nothing to do with his ability to fly his body or land his canopy. It was a tragic, random occurrence.

BMX Hall of Famer Pistol Pete Loncarevich had a different ex-perience, mostly because his accident involved his personal gear. He was going sixty miles an hour when his brakes locked. He flew over the handlebars into a pile of sharp rocks and broke his shoulder. He de-scribes it as "the only injury that scared me. I got up, but I was gun-shy for a year after that when I was going down hills." Top athletes will tell you that managing the fear that Pete had is probably harder than it was for Dan to step out of the airplane after his near-death experience. Even if your brain determines that your maintenance and handling of the equipment were flawless, and that the equipment you are using is the best available, the experience of a problem with it can lead to emotionally crippling "gear fear" that may or may not dissipate over time.

I had to be proactive to eliminate my skydiving gear fear after a minor malfunction. I took an intensive course in repairing and inspecting parachute equipment and earned a Federal Aviation Administration rating as a senior rigger. Having in-depth knowledge of the stuff I depended on to save my life neutralized the gear fear. Learning was my therapy.

Tunnel Vision

Another reason people get hurt is that they are so focused on a goal or a single activity that they lose peripheral vision—literally and figuratively.

Heidi Howkins, one of the world's foremost female mountaineers, has witnessed some astonishing sights, but one in particular seemed like a metaphor for climbing with too narrow a focus on the summit.

> I was alone at night on the North Sister [Cascades, Oregon], climbing by the light of my headlamp. All of a sudden in the scope of my headlamp, there were huge moths on the glacier I was climbing—moths with a three or four inch wingspan. I was at a moderate altitude, maybe 11,000 or 12,000 feet. As I was climbing, I saw more and more of these moths—hundreds and hundreds of them spread across the glacier and frozen into the ice. Their wings

had frozen when they hit the snow. I couldn't figure out what would bring them up that far. I was above the treeline, so there seemed to be nothing that would attract them. Then I realized there was a full moon and the moon crested over the peak. I turned my headlamp off because it was so bright. The entire glacier I was climbing was lit up like a huge light. The previous night, the moon had been almost full and probably the moths had seen the light from miles away and had flown up straight into the ice.

With competitive extreme athletes, this kind of tunnel vision can result from a savage urge to win.

When women's skiercross competition made its X Games debut in 1999, the qualifying skiers were not sure what to expect. In theory they knew because they had seen years of boardercross contests (six snowboarders racing abreast) as well as the men's skiercross the year before. They had some confidence, however, that their event would not be like the 1998 men's contest, which ran on a course designed for snowboarders that could not contain six skiers going at high speed. That mistake had caused numerous crashes and injuries. In truth, they knew that even on a wider course, the proximity to other skiers on turns and a series of closely spaced hills still presented huge risks.

Even so, some of the world's best free skiers and racers accepted the invitation to race. Wendy Fisher and Francine Moreillon have both won the Extreme Skiing World Championship, Kristen Ulmer has skied very tall mountains like Grand Teton, Carolyn "Curly" Curl set the world record in speed skiing, Allison Gannett earned "Queen of the Extremes" in three different countries, Jill Sickles Matlock claimed two national free skiing titles, and many women in the field of twenty had skied some dangerous lines for movies. By the end of the competition, a quarter of them sustained injuries, the least significant of which were deep bruises. Other injuries included five broken teeth, facial abrasions, a torn anterior cruciate ligament, a heel fracture, and a cracked collarbone.

The injured athletes were not upset. They didn't blame each other or the organizers and they didn't complain. They all hit the course focused on skiing to win—speed first, safety second.

Did you ever twist your ankle trying to outrun your best friend at the playground? You may have told your mom it was an accident, but it was tunnel vision.

Ignoring Intuition

You might be surprised to know how many times athletes did not even describe events like avalanches and falling rocks as "accidents." In many cases, they told me straight out that the reason they got hurt was that they ignored their intuition. They disregarded their gut instincts about skiing a line, pulling a trick, or heading out to the wilderness and the results were disastrous. On the flip side, they universally acknowledge that one of the things that keeps them relatively safe in a high-risk environment is their intuition.

After the Nagano Olympics where she won the gold in Super G, Picabo Street went to Crans, Switzerland, for the World Cup finals. The way the papers told it, she realized she was losing control after she tucked to increase her speed on the hill. She slammed into a fence ski tips first and folded up like an accordion. The result was a compound fracture of her left femur and a blown right knee.

Picabo tells a more chilling story—one that invites you to look inward, whether or not you're an athlete.

When I fell and broke my leg at Crans, I knew it was going to happen from the time I got on the plane to fly to Europe. I just had a sense. I had even made the mistake of promising my mother the

night before the race that I'd come home okay. I knew. Everybody
knew. My brother dreamt I came home in a wheelchair. . . . He was
afraid to tell me because it would have made a difference to me.

Picabo had analyzed the course; she kept her mind focused on
the job ahead. But that wasn't enough to protect her.

Her conclusion is haunting and profound. No extreme athlete—
no person who leaves the comfort of home—should forget it: "I was
tuned into the big picture, but I just ignored it. What I'll never do is ignore it again, or think that I can outdo it."

Anyone who thinks that intuition is just too mystical a concept
to incorporate into sports training should consider that athletes of all
different educational backgrounds and cultures believe strongly that it
should influence decision making. Alex Lowe, whom *Outside* magazine
named the World's Finest Climber in March 1999, has an undergradu-
ate degree in applied mathematics and went to graduate school for engineering. But analysis is only half of his decision-making program.

> There are two ways you make the decision about whether or not to
> attempt the climb: 1) Look for the physical aspects of the climb,
> things that threaten like avalanche potential or an ice cliff hanging
> over the route. 2) Just as important is your gut feeling. A lot of
> times your brain will analyze a situation and say, this is a
> reasonable thing to do, but something inside you—intuition—that
> defies analysis, defies reason, says, this is not a good time to do
> this. This is not the climb to do at this point in time. The brain says
> go, the intuition says no.
>
> I think people who survive a long time in climbing heed that
> intuitive voice. People who don't heed it eventually end up in
> trouble.

> **Combine analysis and intuition
> to create an effective
> decision-making process.**

Even though Alex and many other athletes admit to pulling back from an experience because of their intuition, it's often hard to say whether or not something would have happened to them if they'd ignored it. Sometimes, however, facts can validate the feeling.

Scot Schmidt has never been one to back off from steep slopes and highly technical lines. After all, he's Scot Schmidt of Schmidiots fame—the scariest line on Squaw Valley's Palisades at Lake Tahoe, California. So one day when he said no, people paid attention.

> We were in Canada with a group that all wanted to go up into this one bowl and ski this one line. Everybody was getting on their skis, getting ready to go, and I was holding back. One of the leaders sensed that and he said, "Well, let's check it out." He went out and dug a snow profile. After he did that, he realized it was classic avalanche conditions and said, "Let's get out of here." Everyone got the chills. A helicopter came back in and took us away. It was just something I felt. Usually, I'm gung ho. It was beautiful, but it just didn't feel good.

Scot lives by the belief that his intuition is a sixth sense that is "like a muscle you have to exercise. Animals have it. We have it, too. I think we try to be too logical sometimes."

Poor Judgment

Athletes—anybody—no matter how smart or capable, occasionally fall victim to a mistake in judgment that leaves them open to injury. Maybe they should have prepared more thoroughly, maybe they underestimated the challenge, maybe they made a bad spur-of-the-moment decision. No one goes through life without making some poor choices; the question is, how do you respond once you realize your mistake? What do you do to minimize the potential for harm? This is where the extreme athletes shine.

Inadequate Preparation Climber Barb Clemes, a former member of Canada's National Sport Climbing team and now a motivational speaker, nearly lost her life because she and her partner hit a communication glitch they could have easily prevented. She tells corporate audiences about it specifically to highlight the role communication plays in preparing to get a job done right.

Barb was at Lake Louise in Calgary with someone she'd climbed with often. They were going to top-rope a hard route, so they led up an easier route beside it that had a big angle in it. Barb went over to the anchor of the harder route and set it up, then asked her partner to "Take," her order for the other climber to take her weight. Her partner thought she had said "Safe," and immediately made the assumption that Barb was going to set up her own belay and bring her up. This belied common practice for them—generally they wouldn't stay at the top of a climb like that because it's only one pitch long. Nevertheless, they hadn't specifically talked about it in advance.

> When I said "Take" I leaned back. She thought I said "Safe," and
> took me off belay. So I leaned back and I was into a free fall. I yelled
> her name because at first I thought, I'm going too fast. Then I

thought, she's lost control. Then I thought, she doesn't even have me on belay. I began to clutch my knees together and get ready to slam into my feet because at the bottom of this climb was a twenty-foot slab; I knew I was going to hit the slab. Then I was just starting to think, I'm going to flip backward after that and land on my head and I don't have any helmet on.

Her partner reacted quickly and grabbed the rope to try and stop Barb from falling. Friction on the rope from the nearly 90 degree bend in the rock above bought her about two seconds. Suddenly, Barb stopped a foot above the slab. Her partner held her there. They were in shock. The heat of the carabiner used in belaying her had burned halfway through the rope.

Barb had fallen eighty feet. A split second more and their communication error would have been fatal.

Underestimating the Challenge An even more common error in judgment for excellent athletes seems to be underestimating the challenge. Actually, it's common for anyone with ambition to underestimate a challenge, whether it's moving heavy furniture or rewriting a business plan. But when it involves mismatching physical abilities with the task at hand, injury is a likely outcome. In order to avoid this trap, athletes have to tune into slight changes in temperature, winds, their emotional baggage, the fitness of their teammates, and whatever else could affect their performance. It's easy to slip past one of the elements in the excitement of competing or heading out for an adventure. Most athletes readily acknowledge they've done it a few times and, in hindsight, say it was luck, good reflexes, or their guardian angel that saved them from a traumatic outcome.

In Australia, in the 1997 Eco-Challenge, Team Eco-Internet had just ascended out of a canyon. Eco-Internet is currently the only team that has won every major international adventure race. They are renowned for the breadth of their skills and ability to make the strategic and tactical decisions that win a race without unreasonable risks.

All four got off the ropes and started walking out of the canyon. Looking at the map, they elected to take the most direct route to stay ahead. There was a clear alternative, not nearly as difficult an approach as the steep slope they chose, but they saw a chance to gain a more substantial lead. They didn't see the direct route as a great challenge, considering their skills.

One, then another, then a third team member all found themselves on a perpendicular dirt slope that led into a cliff that dropped 1,000 feet down to rocks and a river. Each one stuck a foot in the crumbly, sandy dirt, stepped up, and took a foot out. Each time, where the last foot had been, the path disappeared.

If they had chosen the other route and angled upriver rather than downriver, they would have gone over rocks and boulders and faced an insignificant fall. Because they had chosen the dirt slope, however, they were angled up over the canyon.

They couldn't downclimb, because they had climbed a tree to get onto the slope. They quickly realized that it was an untenable situation. Ian Adamson, an unshakable professional, thinks of this as the worst moment in his racing career: "I had the feeling that I was going to die. I thought, 'Oh my God. I can't climb down. I can't climb up. And if I stay here, I'll just fall off this face.' There was dirt crumbling all around me."

Because they carried packs, there were moments when they were on the edge of falling backward—going past the balance point. It was so steep, they had to plant their faces in the dirt. If they stood upright, just a little bit off the slope, they were in danger of pitching off backward.

Ian resolved not to fall off. He dug in as if he were kicking up a snow slope. Fortunately, putting weight on the dirt compressed it and it became easier to climb. Maintaining three-point contact at all times, he edged his way up the slope very slowly until it was possible to climb out. For the interminable five minutes it took to get out of danger—time does protract in a crisis—Ian had a view of the cliff below.

> That was terrifying for me. Had it just been a dirt slope, it would have been challenging enough, but it fed into a thousand-foot cliff. The three of us were shaking afterward. We were white, shaking. My teammate Jane, who has a great fear of heights anyway—it must have been terrible for her. I kept calling out things like, "It's fine. If you slip down, I'll be behind you, I'll catch you when you come down," knowing full well that if she fell off we'd both fall off and we'd both die. But I just kept saying, "You'll be fine. Just place one foot at a time." She could clearly see what the reality was, but I think my calming, confident voice supported her.

With the mid-afternoon sun lighting the tense climb, the Discovery Channel film crew saw exactly what Team Eco-Internet was doing. Ian remembers that "They dropped their gear, even their cameras, because they knew it was a really dangerous place." Considering that journalists know "If it bleeds, it leads," for the crew to ignore their cameras in a desire to assist was a laudable humanitarian gesture.

The risk the team took didn't even give them an advantage. The fourth team member who did not come with them—they had yelled, "Andrew, don't do it!"—went around the long way and was only five minutes behind them.

Spur-of-the-Moment Decision Acting on impulse, which is so easy to do if you have a passion for your environment, goes hand in hand with underestimating the challenge. The snow, water, rock, or dirt hills can call out like a lover. You have to go—today, now, and right here. And if you do, your judgment may not be the best.

Every extreme athlete seems to have a moment—or several—when the desire to play conquered good sense. Jim Kakuk, captain of the Tsunami Rangers and a veteran of decades of high-risk kayaking, tells a story that captures what can happen when you "just do it" in extreme sports.

Jim was in Mendocino, California, with fellow Tsunami Rangers and huge winter swells. They discovered a spot where there was a small opening with rocks on either side. A tube washed through and into a cave. Gordon Brown, a well-known adventure videographer, went between the rocks and into the cave to shoot. Jim went between them and found a playground—a huge suckhole. In a suckhole, water comes in, then draws out, so it leaves the paddler in a hole at the bottom. Then another wave comes in and fills up the hole again.

Without giving it much thought, Jim ascertained that he could get in that hole and set up for fun, in much the same way that rodeo kayakers do in the river. Conditions were more severe than he thought, however. Currents were rushing out and changing his position between the rocks.

> A wave capsized me and I was in something like a whirlpool from the sheering. I was holding on to the boat. The wave had washed me out. While I was out of the boat, I was sucked underneath. I had a concern about being pushed into the cave. The main force of the wave was out to sea, though. Twice, I went through being sucked in for fifteen seconds at a time and thought, "This is it." The seas were high—eighteen feet. They refracted around the rocks and were about twelve feet high in this opening, but they had the power of eighteen-foot waves because they were focused between the rocks. I felt the suction. It was a hopeless feeling. All those forces were coming into that suckhole.

Jim had been lured to a focal point, where all the forces of the ocean, all its energy, seemed to converge on one spot. It is a most fantastic place to be, but by its very nature it isn't safe.

At one point, his boat was about thirty feet above him getting pushed up on the rock. He asked himself, "Do I want it, or don't I?" He watched the boat. It came right at him. He focused on how to get it because grabbing it could give him buoyancy. This is the moment he remembers starkly—he calls it his "freeze-frame moment" in this event and he maintains that every traumatic episode has one.

At the time, he was trying to do just two things: stay conscious and get pushed toward a side opening. He knew that it was calm on the other side of the rock.

While Jim struggled, Tsunami cofunder Eric Soares watched him in safety. There was nothing he could do to help his friend without endangering himself. From Eric's perspective, Jim's situation was grim.

> It was really bad. The boat went end over end thirty feet in the air and he wasn't in the boat anymore. He bailed out, otherwise he would have come scraping down the cliff. The boat's gone. He's gone. And I'm going, "Oh jeez. I am not going in that cave to get him." I knew he had to get himself out with the backwash. He was getting tired because he'd been in the suckhole five minutes. Five minutes is a long time under these conditions. He wasn't panicking, but he wasn't calm.

Jim chose to stay high on the water, which he says was probably a mistake. He could have gone underneath, avoiding being drawn into the cave and allowing himself to go with the wave toward the opening. He would have been swimming with the undercurrent. Jim remembers that Eric did precisely the right thing: he yelled encouragement like, "You can make it! You can do it, man."

Jim ultimately swam out, got his boat, and counted his blessings.

Eric's reflection on the situation comes back to resisting the moth-to-the-flame impulse. He says, "We should have looked at that suckhole longer. We didn't see what it looked like at its worst. We were taking a risk and should have looked at it for ten minutes or so. You get all excited at the moment and forget to pay attention and grok."*

Jim's freeze-frame moment of seeing his boat shoot toward him during his struggle is a vision that reminds him not to repeat the same mistake he made that day. We all have them. They're like virtual memory pills to help us qualify the urge to "just do it."

Overconfidence

A fifth cause of injuries is what multisport athlete Will Gadd calls the "intermediate syndrome." Most of us call it a simple case of overconfidence. It happens in every extreme sport. In skydiving, it occurs somewhere between 300 to 1,000 jumps. In climbing, it's the second year. It's that stage that is so dangerous for extreme athletes because they have a certain comfort level with the gear and the environment. By that time, they've acquired a cache of "Lemme tell you about the time" stories; people think they're cool. They start to think, "What can go wrong?" or the even cockier, "What can go wrong that I can't handle?" The reality, of course, is that a lot can go wrong and they don't have enough experience to cope with all of it.

One of the best examples of the intermediate syndrome in normal life is driving a car. It hits most of us when we're about seventeen years old and it often results in a fender-bender.

> **You may be born with talent, but not with the knowledge of how to mitigate risk. That comes with experience.**

---

*"Grok" is a term from Robert Heinlein's *Stranger in a Strange Land*. In the book, when someone would die, you would eat him and gain his essence. You would grok him. The term has, therefore, come to mean "process on a deep level."

Facing the Reality of Pain

Sometimes, there is just no way out of getting hurt. A piece of gear breaks or a chunk of rock flakes off and the only question that remains is, "How can I minimize the damage?" A useful answer is often, "Relax." Refer to Chapter 2 for tips on quickly calming down; learn to relax on cue.

Michael Shannon used to lay a nervous body on his luge. He grew frustrated by blowing his starts and feeling anxious on the road, so he started meditating daily. He's sailed off the side of roads since then, as well as had a climbing accident in which he fell thirty feet with slight damage to his ankle. Michael and other top extreme athletes maintain that the key to getting a bruise instead of a compound fracture is relaxation: "Every time I wreck, I relax. It's too late to do anything else about it."

Once an injury occurs, you face pain and diminished ability. If that happens to an athlete in the middle of nowhere or during a competition, the athlete will very likely make the choice to keep moving. For most people, pain is the body's alarm that something is wrong; it is a warning to stop. For the extreme athlete in the midst of an adventure, it's an inconvenience that just makes the going more difficult.

In adventure racing, it's common to see severely blistered and infected feet on competitors who have no intention of quitting. They drain the blisters, apply tape or giant pads of moleskin, and get on with the race. Is that smart? It's a judgment call based on experience. One of my own teammates did it in the Utah Eco-Challenge. He assessed the damage, treated the wounds, and determined they would not cripple him permanently. At that point, he decided the reasons to go on were more compelling than giving his feet a rest, so managing pain became part of the sport.

There are some tricks to doing it, according to the pros. Major adventure races like the Eco-Challenge, Raid Gauloise, and Elf Authentic Adventure last for more than a week, and athletes change terrain, switch gear, and draw on different skill sets throughout the competition. Paradoxically, the struggle and the salvation for a racer is that no one feeling lasts very long. Whether it's the energizing thrill of going downhill on a mountain bike or the agony of trekking on a sprained ankle, the feeling will soon be replaced by a new sensation. Managing pain or sleep deprivation or any of the other elements that are invariably part of an adventure race can be done more effectively if the athlete keeps that in mind.

Adventure racer Cathy Sassin says, "Just when you think you can't stand it anymore, the type of pain changes so you can. Many people who give up, give in, don't realize that." She compares the effort to being in labor. It was one of those things she realized as she was serving as a labor coach for her best friend during the birth of her three children.

> A woman gets to a point in labor where she's going through
> contraction after contraction. It's like no pain she has ever
> experienced in her life. Then the doctor tells her she's only three or
> four centimeters dilated and she screams, "Forget it! I'm not doing
> it! All bets are off! I cannot endure this for fourteen more hours!" So
> you get to that emotional point, but the thing that most people don't
> realize is that you *can* endure it, you just don't know it. Those
> feelings come and go.

Chloë Lanthier-David had to build on that kind of thinking to get through day after day of the 1997 Marathon des Sables, "the toughest footrace in the world." For six of the seven days, she wouldn't have translated it "Marathon of Sand." It was the "Marathon of Pain"— nearly 200 miles traversing unsupported across the Sahara with horribly swollen and diseased feet. On the second day of the race, she started losing her toenails and a severe infection started in one of her big toes. By the third and fourth days, her toes were green and oozing. A skeletal medical crew, equipped with only the basics, correctly diagnosed gangrene and gave her an injection so she wouldn't lose her toes. With that threat under control, her only enemy was the pain.

> The worst was that I had to wake up each morning and keep on running. I could barely walk. We would bivy at night, then wake up at 5:30 or 6:00 to start racing again. I could not put my shoes on, but I had to. I was in the middle of the Sahara. I had no choice. My feet were so swollen that my toes were curled and jammed, plus injured, so it was more than just dealing with the injury. It was a matter of running through the pain. I had tears coming down my face for the first hour of every day, because the pain was so intense. After an hour or so, I would get used to the pain. I would think of something else. The pain would "freeze"—I wouldn't feel it as much—but at night I could barely walk. It was horrible.

Chloë's resolve is extreme by anyone's standards, but her method of coping with intense pain could help anyone. She kept triggering positive responses with simple thoughts like these:

- ◆◆◆ "It's still going to hurt even if I don't run tomorrow."
- ◆◆◆ "I'm proud of myself that I can run through the pain. That feels good."
- ◆◆◆ "Every day, it's just going to get easier because I'm closer to the finish."

Three hundred thirty-nine people from all over the world completed that race. Chloë came in fifth among the 120 women who finished and was the top-ranked North American woman.

> You can decide that pain
> will not be an obstacle.

Since pain management is supposed to be second nature to a good soldier, the United States Army has come up with these instructions for its field manual.

You can tolerate pain if you:

♦♦♦ Understand its source and nature.

♦♦♦ Recognize it as something to be tolerated.

♦♦♦ Concentrate on things you need to do (think, plan, keep busy).

♦♦♦ Take pride in your ability to endure it.*

Based on that formula, Chloë and most of the other athletes in this book are ready for battle.

But no matter what they do, extreme athletes know that, at some point, they will probably get hurt. If they never got hurt or felt pain, they wouldn't be pushing the limits very hard. Franz Weber has a reminder for any extreme athlete: "In these sports, you can't go halfway. 'Just be careful' doesn't work. Crashing, hurting yourself are part of the territory—accept it or leave the sport." As experts and champions, the most they can hope for is that their intuition and good judgment will throw the odds in their favor.

*U.S. Army Survival Manual (Dorset Press, 1991) p. 1–4.

A KAYAKER, A SPEED BIKER, AND A TV AGENDA

Tim Green made it sound like Jamie Simon's next vehicle might be a wheelchair and Carolyn Curl's a hearse. Actually, he was on target. The former football pro was sharing announcer duties with Olympic hero Jonny Moseley for *Extreme World Records*, a 1998 TV special that set up record attempts for four types of stunts and two sports. In the latter category, Curly would attempt to break her own women's speed biking record of 122 miles an hour and Jamie's aim was to plunge down a fourty-four-foot vertical waterfall to establish a women's record in waterfall kayaking.

Setting the speed bike record in 1997 on the same 55-degree track of packed snow in Les Arcs, France, had nearly brought Curly to tears—out of fright, not joy.

> It was the scariest thing I'd ever done in my life. The bike I was given was unstable. It was getting the "speed wobbles"—it flexed to the right and left—it was also fishtailing. I was almost scared to tears, but it was my job to do it.
>
> It was intimidating to see where we were running from. We were a little less than half a mile up this hill. I got out there on the starting platform and one of my French friends named Patrick was up there. He could tell I was freaking out. I figured my eyes were bulging and I was pale. He just looked at me and he gave me a thumbs-up. To me, that was saying, "You're going to be okay." I believed him. I got on my bike. I did it.

She set that record a week after clinching a new women's speed skiing record of 143 miles an hour in nearby Vars.

A year later, Curly went back to try to break her biking record for the TV show. She wore her custom red rubber suit, which helped her aerodynamically, but presented a hazard if—actually, when—she would effect controlled crashes at high speed and slide into the air bags at the base of the hill. Even though the snow was cold, friction from the slide heated the rubber and burned her skin.

Curly planned an attempt to reach 133 miles an hour, which would give her the world record as the fastest human on a bike, not just the fastest woman. Tim warned the TV audience that, at that speed in snow, "braking is impossible and a wipe-out could be fatal." Any logical person watching the cable show would have wondered whether Tim had indulged in hyperbole or Curly was just plain nuts in pursuing this made-for-TV "free fall of controlled terror."

When Curly saw the soft course and bike tires that were ill suited for high speeds, *she* wondered if she was nuts. She knew she really could kill herself if she went over the handlebars and cartwheeled down the hill at more than 100 miles an hour. She did a few practice runs; each time air escaped from her valve extenders so the tires went flat. Each time the bike wobbled. She made it to 102 miles an hour, then nature called off the attempt. Sun made the course far too soft for a world record.

Right then and there, in front of Tim, Jonny, and a TV audience, Carolyn Curl decided, yes, this was a crazy thing to do. She officially retired from speed biking on the spot: "I'm not going to try to break the world record anymore. It's just too risky and I want to live to compete in other sports." She quickly moved on to bull riding.

For Jamie, it was the same show, but a different script. Backed by paddling buddies that included veteran expedition kayaker Scott Lindgren, she chose the site, the boat, and the strategy. She planned every stroke of her ride down California's McCloud River to Biddle Falls. As Tim reminded the audience, Jamie faced "350,000 pounds of bone-crushing water pressure."

First, her team of six scouted a waterfall that was accessible to the camera crew and related production staff—sixty people. They next secured permission from the Native Americans who owned this pristine stretch of forest and river a mile from any parking. Finally, on a clear, sunny day with snow on the ground, snowmobiles transported everyone from base camp to the waterfall to tape the attempt. Jamie prepared to run the river in ways she never had before: "It was the first time in my life I've gone kayaking with makeup on."

> I scouted the waterfall for two days. I knew everything there was to know about it and I knew that once you're above thirty feet, it is much harder to get it right. The higher you go, the more control you lose. There's a lot of risk you assume when you run a drop like that.
>
> You do everything you can to make it safe. I had someone scuba dive underneath to make sure there were no rocks. I rappelled down and looked carefully at the lip of the waterfall. I thought hard about which way to lean—should I sit forward or back or sit up straight. You do everything you can to make sure it's a perfect landing, but when you get above thirty feet, you just have to assume a certain amount of risk because you lose control as you're free-falling. So the more time I had up there, the more time I had to think about all that.

She planned to slice through the water at a 45 degree angle. Tim Green undoubtedly made viewers white-knuckle their remotes when he offered the what-ifs: "If she lands too far forward, she could break her neck. If she leans too far backward, she risks the serious low-back injury known as spinal compression. Paralysis is almost instantaneous."

Jamie splashed some water on her sunglasses and paddled out of the eddy. She put the boat right where she wanted it, felt the free-fall, landed, then came up with a roll and yelled, "That was fun!" She made the record look easy. It wasn't; the announcer had not exaggerated the danger.

> I did not want to land flat. That would have compressed my spine because it was green water. The whiter the water, the more aerated, the softer it is. I wanted the bow to hit first and the rest of my body to flow through. I ended up penciling straight in, which is fine except the body is straight out. It is per-

JAMIE SIMON BLASTS DOWN THE TIERED WATERFALLS CALLED TRIPLE DROP IN THE KERN RIVER IN SOUTHERN CALIFORNIA. THEIR COMBINED HEIGHT IS ROUGHLY WHAT JAMIE FACED AT THE WATERFALL ON THE MCCLOUD, WHERE SHE SET THE WORLD RECORD.

pendicular to the boat. The amount of water that hit my face really hurt. My boat broke the water, but the pressure of the water was tremendous. The lenses of my sunglasses popped out. It was my fault. I wore a stylish pair for the show instead of the ones I normally wear. I had a headache for five days and think I had a mild concussion. I couldn't look to the side; I'd have to turn my whole head. I also cracked a tooth because I bit down so hard. It turned out to not be such a glamorous thing. I had a near-perfect landing and still those things happened.

Jamie had three reasons for going past her comfort level. She wanted to draw attention to the sport and she wanted women to see what a woman in the sport could do. Her third reason was the same as Curly's—it was her job: "I can't emphasize it enough, setting records is not where my passion lies. It's being on the river. But it's projects like this that provide a paycheck that enable me to get back to the river."

That being said, she has one overriding memory: "The whole experience was fun."

When you have a setback, it can be disorienting. You can lose your focus and direction; you can squander your resources. Or, as these extreme athletes learned, you can turn your situation around and be a real hero to yourself. Other lessons extreme athletes offer you are how to avoid the self-sabotage that can lead to a loss or crisis.

APPRECIATING a comeback—a

return to status or safety despite the odds—seems to be part of human nature. We admire actors who reenergize their careers or soldiers who escape from a POW camp. They have faced things we don't want to face like failure, a loss of respect, terror, or hopelessness, but instead of giving up, they reversed their fortune. They collected their wits, created a plan, and moved on.

In sharing their stories, the athletes volunteered what they did to rise to the performance level they wanted after a setback, or what they did to save their lives. Just as important, they admitted sometimes undermining themselves at the outset through wrong assumptions and other lapses we can all relate to, and

CHAPTER 8

SKATEBOARDING LEGEND TONY HAWK PRACTICES IN THE HALFPIPE AT THE 1999 X GAMES, WHERE HE WOULD SOON ATTEMPT THE GREATEST TRICK OF HIS LIFE—THE 900—A TRICK HE'D BEEN TRYING UNSUCCESSFULLY FOR TEN YEARS.

they described ways they learned to avoid that pitfall. One way they sabotaged their effort that may surprise you is with fear—not of a radical stunt or fierce mountain conditions, but a fear of failing to win or to reach the summit.

> **A desire to succeed can strengthen you, but a fear of failure can immobilize you.**

From Loss to Win to History

In 1986, *Sports Illustrated* proclaimed: "In skateboarding's showcase event of vertical riding, there is only one bird worth watching—a high-flying Hawk named Tony."* Tony Hawk was eighteen at the time.

Twelve years later when he showed up to compete in the 1998 Summer X Games in his hometown of San Diego, he had already won twelve world championships, as well as the "vert event"—aerial stunts in the halfpipe—in two of three years of X Games contests. The pressure was on. The crowd was his. The rivalry was familiar. His only competition, so everyone thought, was fellow San Diegan and doubles partner, Andy MacDonald, with whom Tony did a spectacular gold medal run in those same Games. The two traded boards in midair to work the cheering crowd into a frenzy during the world premiere doubles competition.

So when Tony, the perennial king of skateboarding, captured third place, disappointment shot through his fans at Mariner's Point in Mission Bay Park. What happened?

---

*"Chairman of the Board Tony Hawk, an 18-year-old from Southern California, is riding the crest of popularity as skateboarding once again enjoys a revival," *Sports Illustrated,* November 24, 1986.

LESSONS FROM THE EDGE

> I had a lot of expectations at the X Games. I had won the year before in San Diego. It was in my hometown again and there was just a little too much pressure. I really felt that. It was hard to remove myself from that. It wasn't just that my whole family was there. The year before I had had one of my best performances ever, so it was, "What's he gonna do now?" That's all I heard.

Tony was the victim of performance anxiety after sixteen years of competition and more first places than anyone in the sport. In some ways, it was a slide back to a time in his life that most of his fans don't remember.

Early in his career, Tony always had the same stress feelings that scrambled his energy at the X Games. Tricks he knew he could do blindfolded in practice took him down in competition. He'd compete. He'd fall. Eventually, he fell less and less and a legend was born.

Tony swallowed the loss and moved on to the Münster World Championships in Germany. But there it seemed that circumstances conspired against him. First, he had to take a late plane that put him into Germany the night before the qualifying runs. Then the airline lost his luggage—he had a board, but no clothes. He had to borrow gear for practice the next morning. When his gear arrived, he had to hurry back to the hotel, then return to the park to qualify. In spite of it all, he qualified first: "Everything felt right."

Everything kept feeling right. It was a different country, a different contest, and a very different stress level.

> It was more relaxed than at the X Games. There were four runs. My first run, I was fairly conservative, but I did things that I knew would be a little bit harder. A little bit risky, but not too much. The next time, I upped the ante. On the third run, I pretty much tried whatever I could because judging was based on only the best run out of the four. I felt like I'd already put together my best run, so on the third, I just took all the risks and pulled it off.

TONY HAWK TURNS HIS SIX FOOT THREE BODY AND SKATEBOARD INTO A
FLYING SCULPTURE.

He threw in a 720 (double spin), varial 540 (the skater does one and a half spins and spins the board a half), and a front-side caballerial (a no-hands 360, with the skater blind to the ramp at the start of the rotation). It's a trick more commonly seen in a movie, where the skater gets several takes. A lot of the other tricks Tony added to his forty-five-second run were the same level of difficulty—"tricks I generally wouldn't try in a contest, but I felt it was the right time."

He won, but that isn't what made Münster 1998 one of his all-time personal favorite contests. It was because he skated with heart, reaching a performance level that he found exhilarating.

> When I won, I was elated because of my skating. Even if someone else had put something together that the judges decided was a winning run, it wouldn't really have detracted from how I was feeling just from having skated that well. For me, it was just about giving my personal best and it doesn't matter how I've ended up in the rankings if I've skated my best.

Now fast-forward to the 1999 Summer X Games in San Francisco. Tony and Andy once again flew to a vert doubles gold. But Tony had much, much bigger plans because he was "on." In the best trick contest, he went for a 900, or two and a half rotations. It's a trick the top skaters have all tried, but never accomplished. A trick in which the skater spins hard and has to land at the right angle or he will feel like he was in a car wreck. Tony knew—he knocked himself out trying to pull it off for ten years. On his eleventh try, he nailed it. The crowd shrieked and stormed the vert ramp to adore the god of skateboarding.

What can you learn from that? For starters, he "failed" for ten years and even ten times in one night before the headlines blared: 1-900-HISTORY.

1999 WAS A HAPPY YEAR FOR TONY HAWK. HE MADE SPORTS HIS-
TORY WITH HIS 900 DEGREE ROTATION AT THE SUMMER X GAMES AND
WELCOMED HIS SECOND CHILD INTO THE WORLD. AH, THE LIFE OF
A NORMAL, EXTREME ATHLETE.

KIM CSIZMAZIA MADE DELIBERATE STICKS AND KICKS ON HER WAY TO A GOLD MEDAL AT THE 1998 WINTER X GAMES—A FEAT SHE RE-PEATED A YEAR LATER, AS THIS PHOTO SHOWS.

> Peak performances happen
> when the mind and body work together
> at a gold medal level.

Victory Consciousness

Sometimes, you walk into a room and think you're set up for failure. You've never made a good presentation in a room with windows, or it's bad luck to make a pitch after lunch. This isn't a matter of performance anxiety, like Tony's stress over competing in his hometown. This is self-sabotage by superstition—making wrong assumptions about what matters.

Kim Csizmazia spotted that tendency and choked it before the ice climbing competition at her first X Games. She created a competitive advantage where others assumed a handicap.

> I drew first position. I'd been thinking about this and didn't want to go first. I thought it was a disadvantage because the ice isn't going to be picked out. So instead, I just decided, okay, I drew first. I *decided* that was the best place to be. You can make that mental switch. I'm first, that means I'm number one.

A lot of people said discouraging things to her like, "Oh, too bad." And she saw the effect the same draw of first position had on a male competitor, who is well known in competitive and wilderness circles as a highly proficient climber: "I could tell by the look on his face that he let it defeat him a little bit right away."

She made an imaginative leap. The competition was like acting and, no matter what the script, she had the part of the winner. She became that character. She won.

> Competing is like acting.
> Be the character you want to be
> while you are in the limelight.

As it turned out, that year it was even better to go first. There was very little ice over the lip at the top of the tower and each successive climber beat it away so there was even less for the athletes who had the "good" draws.

In the wilderness, outside of competition, seeing promise in the challenge at hand has even more profound implications. Jared Ogden, who has been part of some of the most spectacular first ascents in recent years, adopted Albert Einstein's lemons-to-lemonade motto: "In the middle of difficulty lies opportunity."

In the case of climbing in Antarctica, athletes face an entire continent of difficulty, not just a moment. Einstein's motto served Jared well as he and his teammates Alex Lowe, Conrad Anker, Jon Krakauer,* and photographer Gordon Wiltsie arrived in Queen Maud Land. They went there to attempt a first ascent of the tall, thin 2,000-foot rock tower called Rakekniven ("the Razor" in Norwegian) and found harsh climate and crumbling granite.

The difficulty was clear; Alex summarized the surprising opportunity:

> Instead of some spectacular sunset like you might see in the Alps or
> Himalayas, it's the infinite stillness and emptiness that makes
> Antarctica such a compelling place. Day after day passes and
> nothing happens. When you're down there at that time of year

*John Krakauer's rich, first-person account of the ascent is "On the Edge of Antarctica: Queen Maud Land," *National Geographic*, February 1998.

[Christmastime], which is the Antarctic summer, it's light twenty-four hours a day. The only thing that differentiates day from night is whether you're in the sun or shade. The sun orbits around the horizon, maybe 15 or 20 degrees above the horizon, so it's always light, but sometimes you are in the sun and it's relatively warm, and other times you're in the shade and it's desperately cold. I think that's what's fascinating about Antarctica—the lack of anything happening there. It just makes it so timeless. It makes the rest of the frantic world seem surreal. The tangible passing of time we feel in the rest of the world stops there. It has no meaning.

Something did happen—they reached the summit on the morning of January 3. But after celebrating their victory as the first beings to walk on top of Rakekniven they realized they had to share the glory: Conrad pointed out that there were bird tracks in the snow.

Turn a Difficult Situation into an Athletic Triumph

♦♦♦   Make the attempt with the right people—people you trust, people you like.

♦♦♦   Let the environment guide you—nature will tell you how to succeed.

♦♦♦   Remember why you're there—it's fun, and it's an intimate moment with your world.

Survival Consciousness

In any wilderness situation, it is impossible to have control over weather, the condition of the river, and so on. When you have no practical experience with your team, the variables add up and the odds start going against you. This is what happens on guided trips, where people push beyond their normal limits with the help of a paid expert. They may or may not have the same goal or be able to pull together as a team. They might panic in a crisis. The guides themselves may get overwhelmed and make bad choices.

On Kilimanjaro, the highest mountain in Africa, a guide insisted on carrying sports psychologist Bob Moore's fiancée, Karen Walker, to the summit after her face turned blue and she could barely move. His measure of success was to get her to the top; hers was to climb as long, hard, and high as she could with her partner. Karen wisely disregarded his "help" and went back down the mountain with an assistant guide. Her "survival consciousness" turned her situation around.

> ### Know exactly when it's "too much" if you want to live to tell your scary story. To find out, build your experience incrementally.

Group Dynamics In 1992 during his first trip as a raft guide in Nepal, Scott Lindgren put three boats on an unfamiliar river without realizing he had all the ingredients of a disaster: an approaching storm, skittish clients, and two other underexperienced guides.

> We cut a corner to avoid a spot in the middle of the river. One guide started too late and didn't make it. He flipped in the middle of the river. Six people and all their gear went in, freight-training downriver, while we chased them through white water we'd never seen before.

After a fast chase, Scott counted heads. He had eighteen clients in two rafts. At the start, he had twenty-one.

Two kids from a local village came down to the river and offered to help find the missing rafters.

> Our people were freaking out. One woman that we'd already
> rescued had literally been stripped of all her clothes. She had seen
> God—she had almost drowned half a dozen times. I got all my
> people ashore. I said, "Okay, we're going to divide up. I'm going to
> send two people downstream and two people upstream." But we
> didn't have any idea exactly where the missing people were. Then
> the kids took the two groups through the rice fields and trails to
> search for the others. After about an hour, we located them. They
> had managed to swim to shore.

But the raft that had capsized was gone. And the third guide, who had resumed the trip downriver with his clients, was out of sight. Scott hoped he had pulled over, so he headed down the river to reunite the two groups. At this point, more than two hours had gone by since the accident, the rain poured down incessantly, and it was growing dark on a river none of them had ever run.

On his way to find the other raft, Scott saw gear strewn over the river. As the other guide had turned a corner, a bad move dumped half his people and their supplies into the water. Everyone was exhausted. They had survived, but were still in a dire situation. Tarps, tents, stilts, and other camp essentials had gone downstream. People became hysterical. Locals told them of a village ten miles up a long trail. They did a horrendous hike to the village in the middle of the night and spent the next four days recuperating.

Scott, who was only twenty at the time, had the wits and skill to coordinate survival efforts, but knew he never should have been in that position. He's never repeated the mistakes that made those heroics necessary. Now, he organizes for success, as illustrated vividly by the story of the first ascent of the Thule Bheri (see Chapter 5).

Aside from learning how to make a wild river trip more survivable, he realized something else through this early experience that en-
gendered some wisdom about how far to go with a client or even fellow
boaters.

Most people are uncomfortable with being in an uncontrollable
situation. And the river is uncontrollable, no matter how long you've
been running it. Stuff's going to happen. If you can't live with that,
or if you can't handle it, then, more than likely, you're not going to
continue doing it.

Unfortunately, some people can live with the chaotic nature of
some extreme environments, but can't handle it. Their courage exceeds
their ability. You don't want them to be your guide, you don't want them
on your team, and you don't want to emulate them.

Tips on Choosing a Guide for an Extreme Trip

The company that employs the guide should have:

••• Sound equipment, and the right equipment, including emergency and rescue supplies;

••• High—and specific—standards for its guides (see below);

••• A track record for high adventure, but not recklessness; and

••• A method of screening clients for more challenging trips, for
example, a skiing trip in the background or rafting on a Class V
river. If the only criterion for your acceptance is paying the fee,
find another company. Your life can depend on the ability of
other clients just as much as on the ability of your guide.

The guide should have:

••• A certification, or some equivalent you find credible, that indi-
cates he or she has met certain performance standards, for ex-

ample, a Professional Association of Diving Instructors (PADI) Open Water Scuba Instructor rating;

♦♦♦ Emergency medical training;

♦♦♦ Experience on the particular mountain, river, or other site where you will be; and

♦♦♦ A personality and demeanor you like. Don't take a risk with someone who makes you nervous or gives you a creepy feeling.

Self-Rescue In sharp contrast to a guided expedition, all the people variables that can jeopardize survival vanish on a solo trek. On the other hand, of course, there's no one else to help you.

Heidi Howkins, who has led international Everest and K2 summit attempts, does not reject team efforts on big mountains, but sometimes she enjoys going it alone. Her maturity as a climber makes that a reasonable choice.

In May 1997, Heidi soloed parts of Kanchenjunga to experience solitude and an extreme sense of self-sufficiency. She wanted to test her limits. The third highest mountain in the world after Everest and K2, Kanch taught many people the limits of their abilities. Several attempts to summit "Five Treasures of the Great Snow," the translation of the Tibetan name of this mountain with five peaks, have ended fatally.

> I was in a snow and ice couloir, maybe a 60 degree slope. It was really mellow climbing, but enough that you need two axes, and at 21,000 feet nothing's really mellow anymore anyway. Because I was climbing solo, I had no rope. There was bad weather; it was snowing all around me.

Couloirs can make a climber's trek up the mountainside easier by offering a direct route. Unfortunately, they are also natural avalanche chutes.

Heidi heard a huge crack and the crescendo of snow thundering down. She knew exactly what was happening. At that moment, time slowed down for her. She was beset with an emotional numbness; cold, rational responses took over. She sunk both her axes into the ice to prepare for the worst. There were seracs, or large ice towers, on her right that would be dangerous to go toward. And a steep band of rock on her left made it clear there was no way to climb out of the way of the avalanche. She assumed that the climbers at base camp might hear the avalanche, but that they probably wouldn't notice it.

Avalanches are pouring down the face of the mountain several times a day and even if anyone did hear it, it would be ridiculous to expect help. The nearest climber was maybe seven hours away and the difference between survival and death is more like seven minutes.

Heidi was alone in a very real way. The way time protracts in a crisis like that gave her mind the liberty of exploring a hundred thoughts in a few seconds. She even remembered a passage from the classic mountaineering guide *Freedom of the Hills.* The section "How to survive an avalanche" starts with "Yell to your partners" and "grab a rock or tree" and ends with "If that doesn't work, swim. Stay on the surface by using swimming motions, flailing arms and legs, or by rolling."* So much for good advice.

I remember thinking that was outrageously funny. The concept of swimming with a heavy pack and two ice axes and crampons. Right. The authors are either comedians or very proficient swimmers. Probably I should have trained in a lap pool in the slow lane with two ice axes.

*"How to Survive an Avalanche," *Freedom of the Hills,* fifth edition, ed. Dan Graydon (The Mountaineers, 1992), p. 312.

Then the first chunks of ice hit her. Heidi admits her thoughts got jumbled at this point, but she does remember pain ripping through her head. A blow on her back wrenched her from the holds she had with her ice axes. After that, the snow engulfed her and she was tossed around, as if an ocean wave had swept her away. She lost her orientation after flipping over a few times.

> I landed what I thought was face down, with tons of snow on my back and feeling my chest collapse and hearing air and a groan squeezed out of my chest. My mouth was open. My eyes were open, or felt like they were open, staring into the blackness. Then the panic set in. The knot that starts in your stomach and bubbles up to your throat as your mind is telling your body to move and nothing is responding. That ache that you get when you're out of oxygen. Then just a kind of relaxation and ringing in my ears. Just relaxing and hearing and feeling everything shifting, and turning and crunching in a sort of disembodied way.

A voice, her voice, got loud in her head and told her what to do. It told her to roll over. She tried, but nothing happened.

> There was this ache and flash of light in my eyes and I just lost consciousness. At that point, I could have had one of those out-of-body experiences. The darkness gave way to a bright circle of light. Feeling like there's such an incredible attraction in that light—like a magnetic force—that everything around you in your field of vision is aligned toward it—like you're going through a tunnel where everything is aligned in one direction. I didn't feel like I had any body, just a mind that had that alignment like iron filings. Very direct and unambiguous. So there was this bizarre experience, then all of a sudden, this experience of reentering my body.
>
> During the out-of-body experience I was sure, I just knew, I had died.

Although Heidi isn't certain, in all likelihood a second wave came down. It isn't unusual for serac avalanches to include a couple of waves. Did it toss her back to the surface, or release the snow above her? However it happened, nature, the mountain, had spit her out. Heidi's lungs automatically expanded. She retched, gagged, and puked up pink snow. At some point during this she also had a vision of being in a labyrinth that disgorged her.

For Tibetan Buddhists, Kanchenjunga is the most sacred of the 8,000-meter (26,000-foot) peaks. In fact, when a British climbing team led by Charles Evans came close to the top in 1955, they stopped five feet from the summit out of respect for local religious practices. Among the beliefs the locals hold is that ice caves are passages to another world. The seracs look like ice caves; porters had warned Heidi not to go there.

> Gagging, puking, snow in orifices—eyes, nostrils, ears. Took a while for me to clear everything and when I did, I just rolled onto my back, kind of ignoring all of the pain. There was blood on my forehead. I started laughing one of those crazy outbursts like the hysterical laugh of a mad scientist or a kid playing a prank. Then I started coughing again. I remember squinting up at the sky with snowflakes on my eyelashes and feeling the cold, the snow that was landing on my cheeks and melting—like hot tears on my face. One of those moments when the sensation of being alive was so intense and real. At that point, there was another little spindrift avalanche that brought me back to reality quickly and reminded me I had to get out of the couloir as quickly as possible. I found my ice axes.

Despite the throbbing in her ear (she later found out she had perforated her left eardrum) and a trickle of blood—"it was a real nuisance"—coming down her forehead and into her eye, Heidi had to move on. She had no first-aid kit. Weight is a critical factor in high-altitude climbing without porters. It's not uncommon for a climber to leave the toothbrush behind, so bandages would not find a place in her pack, either. She pressed her head in the snow to stem the bleeding, then began kicking her way down the slope.

At the bottom of this couloir, there was a little cluster of tents. As she was going toward them to see if anyone was there—there wasn't—she saw something in the snow that caught her eye. She jabbed at it with her ice axe. In the flat white light of the storm, she had discovered a khata, a long, thin consecrated white scarf that monks sometimes give to climbers for good luck. She tied it around her forehead.

Heidi settled into one of the tents and slept for about fourteen hours straight. That's a rare feat at altitude, especially without hydrating. Was it just enough rest to return to base camp, or enough rest to go on? The beautiful weather the next morning invited her upward, but she looked around.

I stood in the flat area at the bottom of the couloir and looked up and I must have been there for about an hour staring at this couloir from the safety of the tent, completely mesmerized by the silence and the heat wave floating above the couloir. There was a tower of unstable ice to the side of it—a thousand-foot-high pile of unstable blocks. The slopes were still heavy with snow. The seracs were still unstable and I was still alone. To top it all off I had that nasty cut on my forehead.

I couldn't bring myself to go down. The weather was beautiful and I felt strong enough to climb.

Climbing, like survival, is an instinct, and at that point, every fiber of my body wanted to climb—to go up. Reason and intuition were in conflict and intuition seemed strong. In retrospect, I'd have to say that it was right. The only real reason to go down was mental. There was nothing in my physical state to stop me from climbing, although I couldn't have known that in a rational way. I knew it in an intuitive way.

But nature said, "No, you can't go." A storm blew in and, for the next three days, she had to dig herself out of the tent every two hours.

Heidi did not reach the summit, but on May 15, 1997, she became the first woman to reach the base of the summit pyramid at 8,100 meters, about 26,500 feet. The Dalai Lama's office sent her a message soon after that. Heidi has been invited to climb the sacred east side of Kanchenjunga. She says she will.

The rewards of Heidi's experience are immeasurable—a validation of her physical and mental strength and skill, sharpened senses, heightened awareness of what it takes to survive. It's no wonder she would want to go back. In the words of Mihaly Csikszentmihalyi, author of *Flow:*

> The best moments usually occur when a person's body or mind is stretched to its limits in a voluntary effort to accomplish something difficult and worthwhile. Optimal experience is thus something that we *make* happen.*

*Mihaly Csikszentmihalyi, *Flow: The Psychology of Optimal Experience* (HarperCollins, 1990), p. 3.

THE 7.3-SECOND SKYDANCE

The skydiving community seemed divided into two camps about the world record attempts of July 1998. There were those who thought the naive over-confidence of these 300 skydivers would stink up the sky. And there were those who believed that this mix of elite and B-team athletes could push skydiving to new heights, that they could actually build a single formation that would break the record of 200 that had stood for six years.

For personal reasons, some skydivers even chose to broadcast their disdain for the organizer, Roger Nelson. They posted World Wide Web no-tices warning that he was like the crazed evangelist Jim Jones and before the week was over, everyone at Skydive Chicago would be drinking toxic Kool-Aid.

On Sunday, July 19, those who shared Roger's grand vision put months of personal preparation to the test when they began jumping to-gether in Ottawa, Illinois. Roger and the chief formation designer, D. D. Bart-ley, had posted explicit instructions on a special Web site—all the jumpers knew their precise positions in the formation. They even knew their aircraft and where they would sit in it four months in advance. They also got tips on building their fitness level and skills for the series of twenty-five record at-tempts. In short, Roger and D.D. used the Web in the same effective manner that corporations do—to focus hundreds of people on the same agenda. In the recent past, skydivers would show up at the event and receive a piece of paper or booklet with notes and drawings. They had to do multiple ground rehearsals, or "dirt dives," to get a specific sense of where to go. This time, the dancers showed up for the rehearsal already knowing the choreography. Another organizing principle, used in past world record attempts, was color-coding the jumpers. In this laced formation, loops of jumpers suited in red, yellow, green, blue, orange, and black looked for others with their color or for the white-suited jumpers who joined the different sections.

The attempts began in hot and miserably humid weather. The jumpers boarded planes equipped with hoses going to an oxygen supply that they would start using at around 15,000 feet. These twelve large aircraft—seven Otters, three CASAs, one Skyvan, and a DC-3—would soon be flying in close proximity.

Sunday, July 19

Jump No. 1	Number on Jump:	300
	Altitude:	17,000 feet
	Result:	Unsuccessful

In his logbook, Jim McCormick made a note that his opening altitude was 1,300 feet above the ground (AGL). If skydivers follow Federal Aviation Regulations, they try to have an open canopy by 2,000 feet AGL. At 2,000 feet AGL, a skydiver is about eleven seconds from impact. A heads-up jumper should be able to handle a malfunction at that altitude by cutting away the bad canopy and deploying a reserve. Having a problem below that altitude is, well, a crap shoot. In this case, Jim couldn't get "clear air" because so many bodies were around him. Deploying his parachute in that much air traffic could kill someone, including himself.

Jump No. 2	Number on Jump:	299
	Altitude:	17,000 feet
	Result:	Unsuccessful

Once again, a confused breakoff put many jumpers in each other's airspace at pull-time.

Jump No. 3	Number on Jump:	299
	Altitude:	17,000 feet

Jim succinctly recorded the result of Jump No. 3 in his logbook: "Base funnel, very ugly, horrible breakoff, midair collision and fatality."

Sandy Wambach collided with a jumper named Wally West when he turned to exit the formation. Despite her hard helmet, the high-speed impact knocked her unconscious. Seeing that she was out of control, Ray Murphy chased her low, getting five feet off to her side. At that point, he realized he wouldn't reach her reserve ripcord in time. There was nothing more he could do without jeopardizing his own life. He deployed his own parachute and kept looking straight down as Sandy continued on her final skydive.

The accident was too much for some jumpers; they bowed out.

Jump No. 4	Number of jumpers:	290
	Altitude:	17,000 feet
	Result:	Unsuccessful

Jim's notes indicate that the jump worked fairly well, but his opening altitude, due to the same problem, was 1,000 feet—an unwanted personal record. Others shared his experience.

Just after that, everyone started to follow the new procedures for breakoff that had gone into effect after Sandy's death.

By Thursday afternoon, July 23, the number of skydivers was down to 267 on attempt No. 15. Exit altitude had been increased to 18,000 feet and the jumpers felt some pressure. They had less than three days left to succeed. When they returned to their hotels to rest up for the next day, D.D. once again—she had sacrificed sleep by doing this every night—stayed behind at the drop zone and redesigned the formation for fewer people. That evening, another four underperforming jumpers had been asked to stand down.

Friday morning, Roger decided it was time to reenergize the masses. He asked Jim, a professional motivational speaker, and a couple other vocally optimistic people to help set the tone for the next three days. They pumped everyone up, but before turning them loose, Jim stuck a song into their heads—Queen's "We Are the Champions." It became their anthem.

The next morning, on their twenty-first attempt, 259 skydivers held a formation for 2.25 seconds, earning them a place in the *Guinness Book of World*

Records for the largest free-fall formation ever built. Great, but that's not what they came for. The jump did not earn an official international record because it was .75 second shy of the three-second hold required by the Fédération Aéronautique Internationale (FAI), the world's air sports federation.

Sunday arrived. They had two chances left.

Jump No. 24 Number of jumpers: 246
                   Altitude: 19,900 feet
                   Result: World record

Three judges from the FAI meticulously reviewed the videotape of the 246-person formation. They compared every "grip," or hold, that one skydiver had on another, to the diagram of the formation they'd been given in advance. They timed how long the jumpers held those grips. Ultimately, they officially declared that the 246-person formation held for 7.3 seconds and was a new skydiving world record. There was Kool-Aid at the victory celebration.

THREE major factors will affect the creation and evolution of extreme sports and your opportunity to participate:

1. Audience and sponsor expectations will affect the style and character of competitions and world record attempts. Television and the Internet will, of course, help to meet and shape those expectations.
2. The interplay of human imagination and technology will produce new sports and variations on existing ones. It will also lead to virtual extreme experiences that support wild fun for weekend warriors and training for hard-core athletes.
3. Athletes will keep evolving on every level to raise performance standards and stretch the definition of "reasonable risk."

An Extreme Future

CHAPTER

9

Audience and Sponsor Expectations

Audiences and sponsors expect professional athletes to push as hard as they can. This has primarily positive results. The athletes' all-out efforts lead to advances in equipment, evolution of the sports, and compelling entertainment.

Because top athletes want to push performance limits, they work with their equipment sponsors to fine-tune the gear. On occasion, they take a whole new set of risks by then testing prototypes. Their efforts pay off for the general public shortly after that with enhanced performance and safety features in cars and the mass-marketing of high-performance bikes, skis, parachutes, boats, ice axes, and so on. A mountain bike trail that is too steep and rocky for the average rider one year becomes doable the next year on a bike with a carbon fiber frame, full suspension, and electronics that automatically adjust the bike's geometry for the hill.

Extreme sports fans benefit from the fact that extreme athletes have proven that their sports events can draw massive television audiences. As the athletes get broader media exposure, their value to sponsors rises, so they can actually make a career out of activities that used to just suck up every dollar they had. They can train professionally and be in top form for more contests. In short, they can give their fans more of what they want to see.

Biker Sherlock said his funding spiked when his sponsors realized he would be competing at NBC's Gravity Games, which premiered in 1999. Biker was a four-time gold medalist in luge at the X Games—aired on cable TV—but his stock soared just by having a slot in games planned for network television.

As extreme sports take their place in mainstream programming, TV could:

1. **Push them into even higher levels of risk to grab ratings.**

TV has already tested the waters with shows like the 1998 special called *Extreme World Records;* we will see more programming like this. Sponsors want their athletes who have proven they can set world records to do it before huge television audiences. And sponsors and athletes alike know those audiences will not stop channel surfing for record attempts that look safe.

After their world record attempts for the show, speed biker Carolyn Curl and waterfall kayaker Jamie Simon talked about their efforts being a scary job (see "Lessons in Action: A Kayaker, a Speed Biker, and a TV Agenda"). Curly and Jamie took exceptionally high risks for a paycheck. They admit it, but they also took extraordinary measures to mitigate their risk. That's the difference between a daredevil and a professional extreme athlete.

2. **Do a better job of covering extreme sports as they really are.**

This is a likely outcome now that millions of people, instead of thousands, have had some exposure to skysurfing, ice climbing, and other extreme activities through media coverage. Knowledgeable audiences won't settle for the highlights alone or abbreviated versions of the contests.

Biker Sherlock is one of the many athletes who thinks that coverage of contests as they are done on the circuit—and not redesigned for TV as they commonly are to accommodate short attention spans—will provide plenty of excitement. It's been done for years with Indy car racing. Biker cites road luge contests as a prime example of where this extended coverage would also work.

When luge first came to TV in 1995 as part of ESPN's inaugural Extreme Games (now X Games) in Providence, Rhode Island, a new sport was born. People had been land luging for years, but suddenly lugers accustomed to racing for several miles faced a three-quarter-mile course. The ESPN version has athletes on their backs traveling around wicked turns an inch off the road on eight-foot aluminum sleds at over seventy miles an hour. It involves a powerful paddling start, the ability to control turns, and the willingness to take a high-speed slam into hay bales. Traditionally, however, luge also required keen drafting skills, which don't come into play on a short course. Biker believes that a televised luge event that he helped coordinate in Australia in April 1998 showed that the "real sport" is plenty dangerous and, as such, is great television. Biker:

> It started raining. All the competitors said, "Let's go for it!" The hill was seventy miles an hour. It was more than a mile and it had some radical turns in it. Passing was done as far back as sixth place to first. That was achieved by Pamela Zoolalian in the semifinals. She was the only woman. She got there on her own merits and she ended up being in the semifinal of a six-man heat and went from last out of the push gates to first and pulled off one of the most insane passes I've ever seen right before the finish line.
>
> I myself came out of the gates in a four-man race last—my light didn't turn green—and I passed everyone clean and ended up first. You don't see that in the X Games because it's a half-mile hill. First out of the gate wins.

While television audiences will continue to see extreme athletes push the limits, the shows ultimately will be tame compared to real-time, unedited, multimedia Internet coverage. In July 1999, www.quokka.com offered a taste of the extreme around the clock:

> This website allows you to track the progress of The North Face Climbing Team as it struggles to reach the 20,618-ft. (6,286-meter) summit of Great Trango Tower in Pakistan. See videos and still images transmitted right from the wall. Read the climbers' journals, listen to their audio transmissions, monitor their biometrics, send them email and get updates regularly from Base Camp.

The advantage of TV coverage in the traditional sense is still the production values—editing out the slow parts like climbers resting, adding music and color commentary while they're powering toward the summit, and so on. The advantage of the Internet is the ability to deliver a real-time multimedia experience. The combination of the two will be awesome for twenty-first-century fans who want their event coverage on demand, but also want the highlights well packaged.

Many extreme athletes won't be nearly as delighted. Some struggle to ascend remote peaks, for example, because they are remote. No matter how much sponsorship money is at stake, these athletes will fiercely resist exposing their adventure to the entire planet.

In general, however, I think real-time multimedia Internet coverage has positive effects beyond meeting fans' desire for high performance because of the intimacy that it offers with the experience and the athlete. It will arouse curiosity in more people about physical risk taking and help inspire them to go beyond their normal limits in many areas of their life. Highlights on TV make the feats seem nearly impossible. Watching athletes struggle to achieve them helps us relate to the people, their dreams, and their process of conquering the impossible.

Imagination and Technology

Our dreams tell us we can fly or breathe underwater or climb like a spider and we find ways to do it. And as we develop new technology, we find even more ways to do it.

Building on the Present Extreme sports give birth to other extreme sports quite regularly. Often, athletes use the tools of one activity to create another one, or transfer a technique from one sport to another, or combine activities into multisport events.

In the late 1960s, people thought it was strange to want to surf the snow. Thirty years later, an estimated five million people do it. The

SURFING ON THE SAND.

birth of snowboarding marked an important evolutionary step in sports not only because it illustrated one more way to have fun with a board, but because it helped push skiing in a wilder direction. Freestyle skier Francine Moreillon believes snowboarding taught her "a lot about reading the mountain, the rocks, the jumps."

> Snowboarding gave a big kick to skiing. If you look at the shapes of skis—never mind the attitude and expectations of the people on them—you see that the contour is made for fun. It's all influenced by snowboarding.

In the early 1980s, skydivers started using similar boards to surf the air. Francine and her friends in Switzerland added lake surfing to the roster of board sports in the mid-1990s. While standing on a surfboard and holding a rope attached to a boat, they surf the wake of the boat, eventually releasing the rope and continuing to surf. More recently, some people have tried surfing the sand.

Like boards, parachutes have spawned a multitude of extreme sports from different flavors of skydiving—formation flying, style, skysurfing, and more—to activities focused primarily on flying the parachute. Paragliding grew out of parachuting after the development of square canopies in the late 1970s. At first the pilots flew unmodified parachutes off steep hillsides, then they re-designed the canopy specifically for flight rather than descent. Now Will Gadd, who set the world record in cross-country paragliding, sees a radical next step. He believes that technology will put paragliders nose-to-nose with jets:

> Our wings will get so good that longer and longer flights are going to be possible and we'll be doing those flights at very high altitudes. There's no reason why you couldn't fly up to the middle of a thunderstorm at 60,000 feet and have a cross-country from that altitude. You could also:

♦♦♦   Fly over Everest.

♦♦♦   Fly the length of the Himalayan spine, landing on a high peak each evening and launching the next day to fly another hundred miles.

♦♦♦   Fly over the oceans. There are thermals over the ocean.

Skydiving's latest offshoot is freeflying, which is mainly the brainchild of Olav Zipser. Olav practiced tracking—flying earthward at a high rate of speed—then transferring that energy to a horizontal direction, and doing other experiments with human flight. He did loops, spins, and barrel rolls, angled his body, and positioned his head to the earth with his feet up and his feet to the earth and head up. Meanwhile, many other skydivers thought (and still think) that the ultimate high is building gigantic formations (see "Lessons in Action: The 7.3-Second Skydance") and they get very, very serious about flying "right" to accomplish that. Olav heard lots of people blame lots of other people for screwing up the skydive while he continued to play with flight concepts and analyze what worked. Then, in the early 1990s, he started teaching other people how to have fun and "freefly."

> I imagine freeflying as a martial art. I want people to imagine that every muscle of their body is in perfect control, not matter how tense or how loose they are. Then you need to have a balance. Everything from martial arts, you take that and put it in the air where you can't fall over and hurt yourself.
>
> You create low- and high-pressure areas by maneuvering your body and pitching it in the line of flight.

As skydivers doing traditional relative work, or formation flying, become more and more accepting of freeflyers, Olav sees the next step in skydiving as combining the two. The aesthetic and athletic goal would having freeflyers "swimming" through formations like dolphins.

Photo by Kurt Issel.

IN FREEFLYING, SKYDIVERS CREATE MIRROR IMAGES AND
OTHER 3-D ARTISTRY.

Photo by Tracy St. John.

ROPED TOGETHER, AN ADVENTURE TEAM CLIMBS INTO THE CLOUDS TO THE GLACIERS IN BRITISH COLUMBIA. IN THE DAYS BEFORE THIS, THEY RODE HORSES, SWAM ACROSS A RAGING RIVER, STRUGGLED THROUGH ALDERS UP A MOUNTAIN IN 90 DEGREE HEAT, PADDLED AND PORTAGED CANOES, AND BIKED FIFTY-FIVE MILES.

Extreme activities also move into new territory when they combine with other sports. For the *Extreme World Records* TV special, for example, one athlete snowboarded off a cliff, went into free fall, then deployed a parachute. The event—loosely described as a combination of snowboarding, skysurfing, and BASE jumping*—would have to be done in places like the Alps and Himalayas, where police won't arrest the athlete for reckless endangerment, trespassing, or setting a bad example for children.

Adventure racing, perhaps the ultimate example of a multisport event, continues to evolve by making broader and greater demands on the athletes. A single race can require expertise with radically different environments and equipment. The permutations are endless as the athletes take on new skills and the gear improves.

A Future for Everyone In the early part of the twenty-first century, wilderness adventures and extreme sports contests will take on a new meaning for millions of people because of computer and network technologies. The time is fast approaching when money, weather, and travel will no longer be valid excuses for not pursuing an extreme activity. The same technology that makes that true will allow extreme athletes of all kinds to train through simulation, and even virtually compete against each other. This is not a *Star Trek*–inspired fantasy, according to Dr. James Canton, author of *Technofutures: How Leading-Edge Technology Will Transform Business in the 21st Century.* This is a near-reality called "telepresence" technology. Telepresence is the experience of completely sensing an alternate reality—such as touching the ropes and sensing the pressure of rock underneath your feet when you're not even on a real mountain.

---

*With few exceptions, BASE jumping—leaping off an object, then deploying a parachute—is illegal in the United States.

In a virtual—or synthetic—reality, it will be possible to fulfill your wildest imagination. You can pick and choose your opponent, your sport, and even set the difficulty level. And with the new technology that will enable us to feel, smell, taste digital reality like physical reality, there will be virtually no difference.

Dr. Canton envisions entire athletic societies emerging that have tournaments both in physical reality and in virtual reality via the Internet. He calls this merging of physical and virtual experience "blended reality" and believes that athletes of all levels will be the main drivers behind the accelerated development of this technology and its acceptance.

Athletes Keep Evolving

Scientific training helps a great athlete become a better one. But add to that the effects of genetic engineering and bionic parts and the possibilities for greater risk taking become nearly endless from a purely physical perspective. Just about the same time we start to experience extreme sports through "blended reality," we will probably see athletes enhanced through implants of different kinds and a whole new generation of performance drugs.

Without human spirit, though, landing a 900 or summitting K2 are just terms to describe robotic feats. Many athletes talk about the evolution of their intangible parts as the real reason why they can push the limits so far out, year after year. Risk taking sharpens their senses, expands their minds, and puts them on a fast track to self-discovery. Just when you thought they couldn't do anything more radical, they do something more radical.

Scot Schmidt is candid about what transformed him from a "young kid going for it" to the athlete that many skiers and ski magazines have labeled the world's best extreme skier.

I didn't believe much when I was young. But then, it was kind of weird what happened. I was learning to snowboard for the first time and I got going too fast. I lost control, went off the run and hit a tree. I hit my head really hard and was knocked out for a few minutes, but didn't even know I was knocked out because I didn't see the tree. I thought I just went off the run and crashed and got up, and went back out on the run. Back on the run my buddies were looking for me. They yelled, "Where were you?" "Nowhere. I just went off the run." But I had been gone for about five minutes, passed out in the snow and I didn't know it. Then I couldn't remember what day it was or who the president was, or anything like that so they knew I had a concussion.

After that, I started having out-of-body experiences. It went beyond visions. I went places. One of my first experiences was in a dream right after I hit my head. I have always been interested in crystals—drawn towards them. I had this dream of a crystal. I put it on a table and all of a sudden it grew and turned into a brilliant, white light. I walked over it and looked into it and there was a being in the bottom of it. So I reached into the crystal and it spun around and touched my finger. When our fingers touched, a spark went off—or energy went in—and I came out of my body in my bed. I was flying around the ceiling, going around and around in a circle looking down. Then I woke up.

I started wondering what was going on (because things kept happening) so I read some books about it and found that other people were seeing things that I was seeing.

I've had dozens of experiences like that. I guess I realized that there's a greater side to me. That's when I started tuning into the earth when I ski. Before that, I was just a young kid going for it.

Many of us don't have a single, dramatic moment like Scot's that triggers a transformation, but we can sense that we are changing, improving. And we will continue to evolve for the same reasons the extreme athletes will evolve into better athletes—we want the breakthroughs, we want to do something memorable. As Jim McCormick puts it, "We spend our lives seeking a transcendent experience." From extreme athletes, we will continue to gain insights that can provide us with those experiences.

Appendix A
Extreme Web Sites

Multiple Sports

about.com (home.about.com/sports/index.htm) can help you start exploring the world of extreme sports through current news and numerous links to sport-specific sites.

adventuresports.com contains links to racing associations, publications, outfitters, and instructors.

ESPN Extreme Sports (204.202.129.27/extreme) offers current reports on contests, calendars of events, and TV listings.

greatoutdoors.com is an interactive site featuring chats with great outdoor athletes, gear auctions, and forums in addition to news and guidance on outdoor activities.

mountainzone.com's up-to-date insider reports on contests and events—from the X Games to Everest expeditions—come from Mountainzone's own staff as well as athletes who contribute.

quokka.com bills itself as "a new kind of sporting venue." With real-time multimedia coverage of events, "spectators become participants and world-class competitors become storytellers."

toptenlinks.org/sports/extreme.vote gives you links to a range of good extreme sports sites in addition to a chance to rate those sites.

Adventure Racing

elf-aventure.com, ecochallenge.com, and raid-gauloises.com provide history and coverage of the three long (a week or more) international adventure races.

mountain-quest.com/calendar.shtml has a calendar of adventure races.

Auto Racing

cart.com is the site of the Championship Auto Racing Teams.

racewire.com contains news of all types of professional auto racing.

Biking

The National Off-Road Bicycle Association can be reached via the adventure-sports.com site (www.adventuresports.com/asap/norba/norba.htm), which links to race schedules, tips, and application forms.

USACycling.org is the association site with a broad range of biking news, race calendars, rankings, and membership forms.

Boat Racing, Top-Fuel

Racer Jim Faulkerson's site (www.faulkerson-motorsports.com) is devoted to the design and performance of the world's first twin-drive drag boat.

dragboats.com has links to racers' sites, schedules, and news.

Climbing

Check out *Climbing, Rock and Ice,* and *Bouldering Domain* magazine sites for background on the sport, its personalities, news, event information, and sport-specific links: climbing.com, rockandice.com, and bouldering.com.

everestnews.com includes a list of firsts on Everest plus news of climbs.

Bartley Mountaineering Adventures (www.bcl.net/~dbartley/Mtresume.htm) not only has details of D. D. Bartley's high-altitude climbs, but also has links to other climbing sites, recommendations on schools, equipment, and workout routines for mountaineers.

In-line Skating

The Aggressive In-line Skating page (home.ican.net/~cirsa/skating/agro.html) describes aggressive skating techniques and includes links to the associations and magazines of the sport.

Kayaking

whitewater.org is the site of the Whitewater Kayaking Association of British Columbia, which offers information on rodeos, races, trips, instruction, and facilitates paddlers' dialogue and gear sales.

For a glimpse of the trips, gear, and people devoted to ocean whitewater kayaking, go to www.tsunami-kayaks.com.

Luge

www.teamepic.com/links/links.html is nothing but links to top street luge sites.

The Road Racers Association for International Luge (www.roadluge.org/rail/rail.htm) has good information for new and experienced lugers via a message board and a section on technical tips.

Paragliding

gravsports.com is Will Gadd's site with articles by him, photos, and other goodies on paragliding and ice climbing, including links to interesting other sites.

Skateboarding

skateboarding.com is an interzine with trick tips, events coverage, photos, product review, and information on skate parks.

Skiing, Extreme

atplay.com/x-team is devoted to extreme skiing and includes information on clinics, skiers, and tips from Kristen Ulmer.

Coverage of the World Extreme Skiing Championships in Alaska can be found at www.wesc.com, which includes profiles of competitors and event descriptions.

Skydiving

The World Organizers for Pro Skysurfing and Freeflying composed www.ssiprotour.com/fr.html, or you can go back to basics with the United States Parachute Association at www.uspa.org.

Snowboarding

hyperski.com is an online magazine for snowboarding and skiing that offers travel information and equipment guides in addition to articles.

snwbrdr.com offers the Finnish perspective on the sport as well as rankings, event coverage, and links to the snowboarding associations for different countries.

Surfing

So . . . you want to learn how to surf THE BASICS: www.surflink.com/justsurf/features/learnsurf/intro/intro01.html is a first step toward the big waves.

Other sites for those who want to move toward the edge:

The Educational Kinesiology Foundation's site, www.braingym.org, provides details on the development and application of exercises such as the cross crawl and lazy 8s.

Jim McCormick's site (www.takerisks.com) on the benefits of taking risks includes articles and quotes.

Or, if you're ready to stop Net surfing and begin a more full-bodied experience, enter the phrase "extreme adventures" in a search engine and you will come up with a list of companies that can help.

Appendix B
The Sports

Dozens of extreme sports receive some attention in this book, but the activities of featured athletes are the following:

Adventure racing: Multisport endurance athletes race in teams through remote and wild areas, often involving extremes of temperature and elevation. They must have skills for all types of terrain and water, and be excellent navigators.

Auto racing, Indy Light: Indy Light emphasize team preparation and driver skill through the use of identical race cars, which are about 25 percent smaller than the CART (Championship Auto Racing Teams) Champ Cars they resemble. Relying on 425-horsepower engines, racers reach speeds of more than 190 miles an hour.

Biking

Bicycle stunt, or freestyle bike riding: Competition is done on dirt, street courses, halfpipes (a surface shaped like the bottom half of a round tunnel), or flat courses and it involves riders doing stunts and jumps with small bikes, derived from the BMX model.

Downhill mountain bike racing: Riders race against the clock on extreme downhill conditions. Drop-offs and turns require technical skill at speeds of forty to fifty miles an hour.

Supercross mountain bike racing: Riders race over hills and around sharp turns on dirt or snow; they may be six abreast or more.

Boat racing, top-fuel: Fueled by explosive nitromethane, drag boats with 6,000 horsepower engines reach speeds in excess of 200 miles an hour on a quarter-mile course.

Climbing

Alpine climbing: High-altitude mountaineers aim for summits on the world's tallest peaks, such as Everest and K2.

Ice climbing: In the wilderness, climbers ascend frozen waterfalls and ice on mountains. In competition, they often climb man-made ice towers.

Mixed climbing: The climber faces both ice and rock challenges. A climber expecting mixed conditions will be equipped for ice (axes and crampons), not rock (bare hands and soft shoes).

Rock climbing

Big-wall climb: A technical rock climb that requires more than a single day to complete.

Bouldering: Low climbing without a rope.

Free climb: To ascend a steep rock formation using only hands and feet. As they ascend, the free climbers place anchoring devices in the rock, then attach ropes to the anchors and themselves for protection, but ropes and hardware are not used to bear the weight of the climber or to facilitate upward progress.

Free-solo: A climb with no protective devices.

Lead climbing: a leader trails the rope and a climber below feeds out the rope while belaying, that is, protecting the leader by attaching the rope to a fixed point. The leader eventually places higher points of protection, and takes in rope while the lower climber ascends, removing protection along the way.

Sport climbing: This is a derivative of rock climbing that emphasizes the technical aspects of the climb. Competitions often involve speed climbing artificial rock walls.

In-line skating: The extreme version is sometimes called "aggressive in-line," which involves tricks and jumps on halfpipes or street courses.

Kayaking
River white-water kayaking

Expedition kayaking: Exploring white water unknown to the kayaker, or in some cases, a portion of a river that has never been run by kayakers.

Freestyle or *rodeo kayaking,* also called *play boating:* Involves tricks in the water; this is done competitively as well as for fun.

Waterfall kayaking: Paddling over falls.

Ocean white-water kayaking: Paddlers play in surf zones, through groups of rocks (rock gardens), and in sea caves.

Luge racing (also called street luge, road luge, and land luge): Riders race downhill on their backs on metal sleds that evolved from skateboards. They brake with their shoes.

Paragliding: Pilots use a large canopy designed for gliding to fly cross-country, from one cliff to another, or along a predetermined course. It is done both competitively and for adventure.

Skateboarding: Skaters do high-flying tricks in "vert" competitions in a halfpipe and on street courses.

Skiing

Super G: Skiers race against the clock on a course that is a hybrid of slalom and downhill courses.

Free skiing

Extreme skiing: In the backcountry, skiing what the terrain offers—steep descents, ledges, and so on.

Freestyle: Involves events with the aim of catching big air and doing tricks like rotations and grabs.

Skiercross (skier x): a freestyle racing event with multiple racers on a course with jumps and sharp turns.

Skydiving

BASE (building, antenna, span, earth) jumping: After leaping from fixed objects, jumpers deploy their parachutes. The highest risk is often the height of the object, allowing no time for the jumper to correct a malfunction.

Formation flying: Skydivers create formations with the goal of doing as many as possible in a set time or joining together the greatest number of people. It involves flat, or "belly-to-earth," flying.

Freeflying: With the goal of "3-D flying," the skydivers fly head down, head up, do multiple rotations and other dancelike moves, creating huge variations in speed.

Skysurfing: Skydivers use a board to "surf" the sky and create formations with a partner called a camera-flyer, who contributes to the final outcome both through flying and artistically videotaping the skydive.

Snowboarding

Freeriding

> *Freeriding:* competitive events with the aim of catching big air and do-ing tricks like rotations and grabs. In the wilderness, freeriding is analagous to extreme skiing.

> *Boardercross* (boarder x): a freeriding racing event with multiple racers on a course with jumps and turns.

Surfing, big wave: Surfers ride twenty-foot or higher waves on long boards, both competitively and for fun.

Appendix C
The Athletes

Athletes mentioned in the book are listed here with distinguishing information relevant to stories in this book. Asterisks denote athletes interviewed for the book, whose experiences and thoughts shaped the "lessons from the edge."

Ian Adamson*—A world record kayaker and member of Eco-Internet, the only team to win all major international adventure races.

Conrad Anker—Along with climbers Alex Lowe, Jon Krakauer, and Gordon Wiltsie, credited with a first ascent of Rakekniven in Antarctica.

J. P. Auclair—A top Freeskier and competitor in premiere X Games Big Air contest.

Waldo Autry—A veteran of street luge competition, considered among the best.

Cullen Barker—An endurance athlete who competes in the annual Iditabike Extreme.

D. D. Bartley*—A world-record skydiver and high-altitude mountaineer.

Jeff Bechtel—Best known as free-climber Todd Skinner's right-hand man on first ascents in the Himalaya and in Greenland.

Brian Boitano*—1988 Olympic gold medalist in figure skating.

Dan Brodsky-Chenfeld*— Member of the world champion skydiving team Arizona Airspeed.

Donna Casey—1992 Kayak Surfing world champion.

Greg Child—Climber/author credited with many first ascents, including the Great Sail Peak on Baffin Island, done with Alex Lowe, Jared Ogden, and Mark Synnott.

Helgi Christensen*—Competitive and wilderness ice climber.

Seung-Kwon Chung—Competitive ice climber and high-altitude mountaineer.

Jeff Clark*—Big-wave surfer who introduced the surfing world to the notorious Maverick's break.

Kirsten Clark—Member, U.S. Ski Team.

Barb Clemes'—A former member of Canada's National Sport Climbing team, and the first Canadian woman to climb a 5.12.

Kim Csizmazia'—Winner of Survival of the Fittest and many ice climbing contests, including the X Games and events at the Ouray Ice Craft Invitational Exhibition.

Mike Curiak—An endurance athlete who competes in the annual Iditabike Extreme.

Carolyn Curl'—World record speed biker and speed skier and competitive bull rider.

J. F. Cusson—Champion free skier and winner of premiere X Games Big Air Contest.

Steph Davis'—A versatile climber whose ascents have included Shipton Spire and Fitzroy in Patagonia.

Vincent Dorion—Champion free skier and bronze medalist at premiere X Games Big Air Contest.

Lieutenant Commander Mark Dunleavy'—Pilot with the U.S. Navy Blue Angels.

Arlo Eisenberg'—Pioneer in what used to be called aggressive in-line skating.

Jarret Ewanek'—Top finisher in speedboarding and street luge who also designs downhill racing equipment.

Jim Faulkerson'—Top-fuel boat racer and designer/builder of new type of top-fuel boat.

Wendy Fisher'—World champion extreme skier and former Olympian.

Charlie Fowler—Climber who attempted a new route on Fitzroy with Steph Davis.

Gerard Fusil'—Best known as the organizer of the Raid Gauloises and Elf Authentic Adventure expedition races, also holds a sailing world record.

Will Gadd'—World record holder in cross-country paragliding, winner of many ice climbing events, and credited with putting up the highest-rated mixed routes.

Allison Gannett—Champion extreme skier and competitor in premiere women's skiercross event at 1999 Winter X Games.

Mercedes Gonzalez'—Winner of nine national titles in women's motocross and a top downhill mountain biker.

Stevie Haston—Pioneer in mixed climbing.

Tony Hawk˙—Perennial world champion skateboarder credited with many bold tricks.

Eric Henrion—Veteran of international adventure races.

Heidi Howkins˙—High-altitude mountaineer who led a 1998 K2 summit attempt and soloed parts of Kanchenjunga above 21,000 feet.

Jamling Tenzing Norgay˙—Member of the IMAX team who summitted Everest in 1996.

Jack Jeffries—Member of the world champion skydiving team Arizona Airspeed.

Jim Kakuk˙—Cofounder of Tsunami Rangers, pioneers in extreme sea kayaking.

Mark Kirkby—Member of the world champion skydiving team Arizona Airspeed.

Franz Klammer—1976 Olympic gold medalist in downhill skiing.

Jon Krakauer—Climber/author credited with a first ascent of Rakekniven in Antarctica along with Alex Lowe, Conrad Anker, and Gordon Wiltsie.

Chloë Lanthier-David˙—An endurance athlete highly ranked internationally for ultradistance foot and bike races and the first woman to finish the Iditabike Extreme.

T. J. Lavin˙—Freestyle bike champion whose victories include a gold medal at the X Games.

Scott Lindgren˙—Expedition kayaker who made the first descent of Thule Bheri in Nepal.

Pistol Pete Loncarevich˙—BMX Hall of Famer and mountain biking champion.

Alex Lowe˙—Big-wall climber credited with many first ascents, including Rakekniven in Antarctica and Great Sail Peak on Baffin Island.

Andy MacDonald˙—Champion skateboarder whose wins have included X Games vert events, including the premiere doubles event with Tony Hawk.

Hermann Maier—Winner of two gold medals in skiing at the 1998 Olympics in Nagano.

Tom Mason˙—Holder of speed world record in street luge and top luge competitor.

Jim McCormick˙—World record skydiver, professional exhibition jumper, and motivational speaker focusing on risk taking.

Casey Mears˙—A top racer on the Indy Light circuit.

Clint Mears—A top racer on the Indy Light circuit with his cousin Casey.

Dave Mirra˙—Bike stunt champion who set the record for most gold medals at a single X Games.

Francine Moreillon˙—World champion extreme skier.

Jonny Moseley˙—1998 Olympic gold medalist in freestyle skiing.

Robert Nagle˙—An endurance athlete and member of Team Eco-Internet, the only team to win all major international adventure races.

Roger Nelson—World record skydiver and organizer of the 246-way world record skydiving formation.

Pat Norwil—Endurance racer; a top finisher in Iditabike Extreme.

Jared Ogden˙—Competitive ice climber and big-wall climber credited with first ascents such as Great Sail Peak, with Greg Child, Alex Lowe, and Mark Synnott.

Shaun Palmer—Perennial victor in snowboarding and mountain biking competitions.

Steve Peat˙—World champion downhill mountain bike racer.

Glen Plake—An extreme skiing champion known for bringing fun to the slopes.

Sammy Popov˙—Skysurfing half of the nationally ranked team Double Trouble.

Dean Potter—Climber who nearly completed a free solo climb on Half Dome in Yosemite National Park.

Dean Ricci˙—Camera-flying half of nationally ranked Team Flyaway.

Dave Rogers˙—Competitive street luger and luge designer.

Gary Ryan—Climber most known for his route called Bladerunner in Rocky Mountain National Park.

Cathy Sassin˙—One of the world's best adventure racers and a member of top-ranked teams in all the major international races.

Scot Schmidt˙—A pioneer in extreme skiing and consistently one of the world's best.

Michael Shannon˙—Veteran luger, successful competitor, and contest organizer.

Biker Sherlock'—Downhill skateboarding and luge champion, as well as a luge event organizer.

Jill Sickles Matlock—Champion extreme skier and competitor in premiere women's skiercross event at 1999 Winter X Games.

Jamie Simon'—World champion rodeo kayaker and world record holder in women's waterfall kayaking.

Todd Skinner'—Big-wall climber credited with many first ascents including Trango Tower in the Himalaya and Ulamertorsuaq in Greenland.

Raphael Slawinski'—Competitive ice climber who has also put up many hard routes in Canada's wilderness.

Eric Soares'—Cofounder of Tsunami Rangers, pioneers in extreme sea kayaking.

John Stamstad—An endurance athlete and winner of the Iditabike Extreme.

Picabo Street'—World champion downhill skier who claimed a gold medal in the Super G in the 1998 Olympics in Nagano and a silver medal in the Lillehammer Olympics.

Rat Sult'—Street luge and snow mountain biking champion.

Mark Synnott—Big-wall climber credited with first ascents, such as Great Sail Peak, with Jared Ogden, Greg Child, and Alex Come.

Candide Thovex—Emerging star in freestyle skiing.

Mary Tortomasi'—Skysurfing half of the nationally ranked Team Flyaway.

Kristen Ulmer'—Most known for skiing stunts in movies and the first female descent of Grand Teton and other tall mountains.

Kirk Verner—Member of the world champion skydiving team Arizona Airspeed.

Steve Verner'—Camera-flying half of the nationally ranked team Double Trouble.

Franz Weber'—World record speed skier.

Gordon Wiltsie—Climber/photographer credited with a first ascent of Rakekniven in Antarctica along with Alex Lowe, Conrad Anker, and Jon Krakauer.

Louis Zamora'—Emerging star in in-line skating.

Olav Zipser'—Pioneer of freeflying.

Pamela Zoolalian'—Top female street luger.

About the Author

Maryann Karinch is the coauthor of *Boot Camp* (Simon & Schuster, 1999) and the author of *Telemedicine: What the Future Holds When You're Ill* (New Horizon Press, 1994). She was one of the few women to complete the inaugural Eco-Challenge in Southern Utah, has logged 650 skydives, is a certified scuba diver, and an avid ocean whitewater kayaker. Certified in personal training by the American Council on Exercise (ACE), she has also earned honors as a collegiate gymnast and amateur bodybuilder. She holds bachelor's and master's degrees in speech and drama from the Catholic University of America in Washington, D.C. She resides in Half Moon Bay, California.

Printed in the United States
By Bookmasters